To M♡ ~~S0-AZA-499~~

Happy birthday
& thanks for
warm welcomes!

Love from
Andrée & Henri

1983

SMALL *Oxford* BOOKS

GUESTS & HOSTS

SMALL *Oxford* BOOKS

❧

GUESTS & HOSTS

❧

Compiled by
MARI PRICHARD

Oxford New York Toronto Melbourne
OXFORD UNIVERSITY PRESS
1981

Oxford University Press, Walton Street, Oxford OX2 6DP

London Glasgow New York Toronto
Delhi Bombay Calcutta Madras Karachi
Kuala Lumpur Singapore Hong Kong Tokyo
Nairobi Dar es Salaam Cape Town
Melbourne Wellington

and associate companies in
Beirut Berlin Ibadan Mexico City

British Library Cataloguing in Publication Data

Guests and hosts. — (Small Oxford books).
1. Hospitality — Literary collections
I. Prichard, Mari
809'.93355   PN6071.H7/   80-42094
ISBN 0-19-214115-5

Printed in Great Britain by
Hazell Watson & Viney Limited
Aylesbury, Bucks

Introduction

This is a bedside book; one for a guest to find beside his bed either as a hint at his own proper behaviour, or to console him for the inadequacy of his host's. It is about the ritual of hospitality, the age-old code that a guest becomes one of his host's family, whether close friend or perfect stranger, and must be given the best. But the tension between good form and the host's or guest's personal inclinations is just as old, and produces endless comedy. This book is an attempt to bring some of that comedy together in one place, and it owes its birth to one guest in particular.

He was an entirely amiable young man who mentioned that he would like to come and see our part of the world. 'Of course, come and stay,' we said. 'Great,' he answered, 'how if I come for a month in the summer?' By then it was too late to do anything but tinker with a disaster. Once an invitation, however casual, is accepted, every scene from arrival to departure has to be played with more or less formality; only the boldest rule-breakers can escape, and we were not that. Since very few people with more time on their hands than oneself continue to seem amiable, we very soon disliked our visitor and dreaded entertaining him. We planned trips he could take on his own, but our hearts would sink when we came home – and smelt his tobacco, or heard the lavatory flush. He always came back early. His sins, the hours he kept, the way he made his bed, his monologues, became our main topic of conversation with other friends. Whereupon we discovered that everyone else had their own store of anecdotes of hosts and guests.

Two friends told us of their more than comfortably-off guest who started a week's holiday with his wife – their honeymoon, in fact – by promising his hosts (our friends) a meal at the best local restaurant. As the week wore on, he made worried remarks about the likely cost; so the meal was re-booked at a more ordinary eating-place. On the evening of the dinner, when the bill came, he leant towards his hosts and asked: 'How much is *my* half?'

One archetypally unfortunate guest was said to have begun his visit to some grand house by arriving at the wrong time. He was shown into the drawing-room to wait, and sat heavily on the sofa. When he got up to greet his hostess he found beneath him the dead body of her chihuahua, which he hurriedly covered with a cushion. During the night, having missed being shown 'the geography of the house', he used a chamberpot, and in the morning he decided to empty it himself out of the bedroom window. Unfortunately the pot parted company from its handle; he heard a crash of glass, and, looking down, saw that the pot and its contents had gone through the conservatory roof below, and had landed on a table laid for breakfast.

For some reason, hosts were more often figures of fun in these stories than guests. One friend bitterly remembered going to a party where most of the guests were middle-aged academics, and the host produced nothing to eat and nothing to drink, and organized a series of party games for the whole evening. Another friend told of the wife of the master of a Cambridge college, who simply *forgot* that she had asked sixty people to a cocktail party, and went out. The following day, she called on all the guests to apologize, and to present each with a pot plant. Another Cambridge lady, when asked to put up some guests during a conference, was reported to have replied: 'Yes, I can take three, provided at least two of them are of the same sex.' Yet another decorous hostess once approved a woman friend of ours for not taking a banana from the fruit bowl. 'Ladies', she said, 'should not eat bananas.'

Books turned out to be just as comforting. The first literary figure to appeal to our guest-beleaguered state was Levin in *Anna Karenina*, coping with his uninvited guest Vasenka, who wears an absurd hat, flirts with Levin's wife, and nearly shoots his host by accident. The household's shock at Levin's impropriety when he sends Vasenka packing, and then their growing relief, are a delight. Literature, in fact, abounds in descriptions of guests and hosts, their human, comic behaviour, and their muddled attitudes to each other, all of which seemed to justify this book.

It contains, however, only a fraction of the possible material. The difficulty of making short extracts out of some of the memorable appearances of guests and hosts accounts for some omissions, my ignorance for more. With a very few exceptions I have not included extracts from plays, from foreign literature, or from folk-tales or mythology. The wealth of anthropological and other serious writing on hospitality is not represented. And I have mixed fact and fiction indiscriminately, for they are performing the same task of reporting on the inherently tense relationships between guest and host, and recording its hypocrisies, its farcical situations, its failures, and its occasional successes.

In every human being one or the other of these two instincts is predominant: the active or positive instinct to offer hospitality, the negative or passive instinct to accept it. And either of these instincts is so significant of character that one might well say that mankind is divisible into two great classes: hosts and guests.

Max Beerbohm, *Hosts and Guests*, 1920

Motives

In most hospitality, free choice and obligation are hopelessly entangled. But when there is, apparently at least, some freedom in the matter, the motives of the guest or host become interesting. Here is a selection.

Let me smile with the wise, and feed with the rich.
Samuel Johnson, in Boswell's Life, 1791

He that would have fine guests, let him have a fine wife.
Ben Jonson, The Poetaster, 1601

Are the motives *pure* which induce your friends to ask you to dinner? This has often come across me. Does your entertainer want something from you? For instance, I am not of a suspicious turn; but it *is* a fact, that when Hookey is bringing out a new work, he asks the critics all round to dinner; that when Walker has got his picture ready for the Exhibition, he somehow grows exceedingly hospitable, and has his friends of the press to a quiet cutlet and a glass of Sillery. Old Hunks, the miser, who died lately (leaving his money to his housekeeper), lived many years on the fat of the land, by simply taking down, at all his friends', the names and Christian names *of all the children*. But though you may have your own opinion about the hospitality of your acquaintances; and though men who ask you from sordid motives are most decidedly Dinner-giving Snobs, it is best not to inquire into their motives too keenly. Be not too curious about the mouth of a gift-horse. After all, a man does not intend to insult you by asking you to dinner.
William Makepeace Thackeray, The Book of Snobs, 1847

Daisy Ashford was a child of nine when she wrote what is in large measure a comedy of guests' and hosts' manners. Bernard Clark is a gentleman, Mr Salteena not quite.

Perhaps my readers will be wondering why Bernard Clark had asked Mr Salteena to stay with him. He was a lonely man in a remote spot and he liked peaple and partys but he did not know many.

Daisy Ashford, *The young visiters; or, Mr. Salteenas plan,* 1919

VERS DE SOCIÉTÉ

My wife and I have asked a crowd of craps
To come and waste their time and ours : perhaps
You'd care to join us ? In a pig's arse, friend.
Day comes to an end.
The gas fire breathes, the trees are darkly swayed.
And so *Dear Warlock-Williams : I'm afraid—*

Funny how hard it is to be alone.
I could spend half my evenings, if I wanted,
Holding a glass of washing sherry, canted
Over to catch the drivel of some bitch
Who's read nothing but *Which*;
Just think of all the spare time that has flown

Straight into nothingness by being filled
With forks and faces, rather than repaid
Under a lamp, hearing the noise of wind,
And looking out to see the moon thinned
To an air-sharpened blade.
A life, and yet how sternly it's instilled

All solitude is selfish. No one now
Believes the hermit with his gown and dish
Talking to God (who's gone too); the big wish
Is to have people nice to you, which means
Doing it back somehow.
Virtue is social. Are, then, these routines

Playing at goodness, like going to church?
Something that bores us, something we don't do well
(Asking that ass about his fool research)
But try to feel, because, however crudely,
It shows us what should be?
Too subtle, that. Too decent, too. Oh hell,

Only the young can be alone freely.
The time is shorter now for company,
And sitting by a lamp more often brings
Not peace, but other things.
Beyond the light stand failure and remorse
Whispering *Dear Warlock-Williams: Why, of course—*
Philip Larkin, from *High Windows*, 1974

THE FLIGHT FROM TOWN

The Invitation

To an Edwardian garden party:

Invitations are sent on a large square 'At Home' card in the name of the hostess about three weeks before the appointed day. After the name of the guest add 'and party,' and in one corner write 'tennis', 'archery', &c ...
Everybody's Everyday Reference Book, 1905

Since much of the comedy of invitations comes from their being false or unwelcome, here first is an example of the entirely genuine and informal. The poet Cowper has invited his great friend Lady Hesketh to stay, albeit at a house specially rented for her near his own at Olney. 'Mrs U.' is Mrs Unwin, the widow to whom he was devoted, but never married.

Mrs U. has bought you six ducks, and is fatting them for you. She has rummaged up a coop that will hold six chickens, and designs to people it at the first opportunity ... Thus, my dear, are all things in the best train possible, and nothing remains but that you come and show yourself. Oh, that moment! Shall we not both enjoy it? That we shall.
William Cowper, letter to Lady Hesketh, 1786

Mr Soapy Sponge, a professional guest, was the invention of the Victorian humorist R. S. Surtees (creator also of Jorrocks, the sporting grocer). Sponge is a penniless adventurer out to cut a figure as a rich hunting man and desirable guest. He meets his first victim at the fashionable resort of Laverick Wells.

Among the many strangers who rushed into indiscriminate friendship with our hero at Laverick Wells, was Mr Jawleyford, of Jawleyford Court, in ——shire. Jawleyford was a great humbug. He was a fine, off-hand, open-hearted, cheery sort of fellow, who was always delighted to see you, would start at the view, and stand with open arms in the middle of the street, as though quite overjoyed at the meeting. Though he never gave dinners, nor anything where he was, he asked everybody, at least everybody who did give them, to visit him at Jawleyford Court. . . .

'Mr Sponge,' said he, getting our hero by both hands in Culeyford's Billiard Room, and shaking them as though he could not bear the idea of separation; 'my dear Mr Sponge,' added he, 'I grieve to say we're going to-morrow; I had hoped to have stayed a little longer, and to have enjoyed the pleasure of your most agreeable society.' (This was true; he would have stayed, only his banker wouldn't let him have any more money.) 'But, however, I won't say adieu,' continued he; 'no, I *won't* say adieu! I live, as you perhaps know, in one of the best hunting countries in England . . . and I flatter myself, if you once come down, you will be inclined to repeat your visit; at least, I hope so.'

Mr Sponge, albeit with a considerable cross of the humbug himself, and one who perfectly understood the usual worthlessness of general invitations, was yet so taken with Mr Jawleyford's hail-fellow-well-met, earnest sort of manner, that, adopting the convenient and familiar solution in such matters, that there is no rule without an exception, concluded that Mr Jawleyford *was* the exception, and really meant what he said. . . . Accordingly, he penned the following epistle:—

'Bantam Hotel, Bond Street, London.
'Dear Jawleyford,

'I purpose being with you to-morrow, by the express

[5]

train, which I see, by Bradshaw, arrives at Lucksford a quarter to three. I shall only bring two hunters and a hack, so perhaps you could oblige me by taking them in for the short time I shall stay . . .'

'Curse the fellow!' exclaimed Jawleyford, nearly choking himself with a fish bone, as he opened and read the foregoing at breakfast. . . .

'Well, but, my dear, I daresay you asked him,' observed Mrs Jawleyford.

Jawleyford was silent, the scene in the billiard-room recurring to his mind.

'I've often told you, my dear,' continued Mrs Jawleyford, kindly, 'that you shouldn't be so free with your invitations if you don't want people to come; things are very different now to what they were in the old coaching and posting days, when it took a day and a night and half the next day to get here, and I don't know how much money besides. You might then invite people with safety, but it is very different now, when they have nothing to do but put themselves into the express train and whisk down in a few hours.'

'Well, but, confound him, I didn't ask his horses,' exclaimed Jawleyford.

R. S. Surtees, *Mr Sponge's Sporting Tour*, 1853

Orphaned, sophisticated, Flora Poste in Cold Comfort Farm *also intends to survive entirely on other people's hospitality. At the beginning of the book she writes to four of her relations asking to stay, and now, with her friend Mrs Smiling, she goes through the replies. Aunt Gwen's and Mr McKnag's offers do not appeal; Aunt Gwen's invitation was to share a bedroom with Peggy, 'so keen on her Guiding'. Flora reads the third letter.*

Her mother's cousin in South Kensington said that she would be very pleased to have Flora, only there was a little difficulty about the *bedroom*. Perhaps Flora would not mind using the large attic, which was now used as a meeting-room for the Orient-Star-in-the-West Society on Tuesdays, and for the Spiritist Investigators' League on Fridays. She hoped that Flora was not a *sceptic*, for manifestations sometimes occurred in the attic, and even a trace of scepticism in the atmosphere of the room spoiled the conditions, and prevented phenomena, the observations of which provided the Society with such valuable evidence in favour of Survival. Would Flora mind if the parrot kept his corner of the attic? He had grown up in it, and at his age the shock of removal to another room might well prove fatal.

'Again, you see, it means sharing a bedroom,' said Flora. 'I do not object to the phenomena, but I do object to the parrot.'

'*Do* open the Howling one,' begged Mrs Smiling, coming round to Flora's side of the table.

The last letter was written upon cheap lined paper, in a bold but illiterate hand:

Dear Niece,

So you are after your rights at last. Well, I have expected to hear from Robert Poste's child these last twenty years.

Child, my man once did your father a great wrong. If you will come to us I will do my best to atone, but you must never ask me what for. My lips are sealed.

We are not like other folk, maybe, but there have always been Starkadders at Cold Comfort, and we will do our best to welcome Robert Poste's child.

Child, child, if you come to this doomed house, what is to save you? Perhaps you may be able to help us when our hour comes.

Yr. affec. Aunt,
J. STARKADDER

Flora and Mrs Smiling were much excited by this

unusual epistle. They agreed that at least it had the negative merit of keeping silence upon the subject of sleeping arrangements.

Stella Gibbons, *Cold Comfort Farm*, 1932

Sleeping arrangements are one of the few weapons with which the inhospitable can actually ward off, rather than merely harass, their guests. I have heard of a man who entirely redesigned his house so as to have no spare room and thus prevent a particular person staying. The following example of the same ploy is quoted in Harold Acton's Memoir of Nancy Mitford. She enjoyed translating her address, Rue Monsieur in Paris, as 'Mr Street' or 'Mr'.

With infinite cunning I have made it impossible to have anybody to stay at Mr because the only way into the bathroom is through my bedroom. Perhaps I could have you however – I'm arranging a little summer bedroom the other side of the bathroom.

Nancy Mitford, letter to Mrs Hammersley

The art of declining invitations by choice must also be represented, rarely practised though it is. In the first example, David Copperfield is being tactful for the benefit of the delightful, but proverbially improvident, Mr Micawber. Margot Asquith and Lord Charles Beresford are the sort of brazen rule-breakers normally only found among aristocrats, who say, or are said to say, what the rest of us only wish.

Mr Micawber was very anxious that I should stay to dinner. I should not have been averse to do so, but that I imagined I detected trouble, and calculation relative to the extent of the cold meat, in Mrs Micawber's eye. I therefore pleaded another engagement; and observing that Mrs Micawber's spirits were immediately lightened, I resisted all persuasion to forego it.

Charles Dickens, *David Copperfield*, 1849-50

Of Margot Asquith:

Amongst the Margot anecdotes was her saying to the butler, on receipt of a telephone invitation to go over to Blenheim for lunch, 'Tell them I would rather *die* than come.'

Lady Cynthia Asquith, *Diaries 1915–18*

Very sorry can't come. Lie follows by post.

Lord Charles Beresford (1846–1919), telegram to the Prince of Wales after an eleventh-hour summons to dine.

THE WARM WELCOME

Arrival

Time is like a fashionable host,
That slightly shakes his parting guest by th'hand;
And with his arms out-stretched, as he would fly,
Grasps in the comer.

Shakespeare, Troilus and Cressida, 1609

The first of the host's resources when receiving his guests is his management of their time of arrival. Joyce Grenfell remembers the poet Walter de la Mare using this ploy with unusual precision.

The first time I went to tea with him I was bidden for 3.45. At 4 o'clock Lady Hamilton, wife of another poet, Rostrever Hamilton, arrived and looked surprised at finding me sitting there. At 4.15 Lady Cynthia Asquith rang the bell and when she saw two of us established on a sofa she looked even more surprised. It amused me to discover that we had all been given different arrival times; I had the longest with the dear man and felt very favoured.

Joyce Grenfell Requests the Pleasure, 1976

For the extreme of failure to manage an arrival, here is part of Dacre Balsdon's despairing portrait of a don's wife in North Oxford doing her duty as hostess. The guests are to be two undergraduates and an American Rhodes scholar by the name of Larry Minthauser.

From the envelope Larry expected something more interesting, and so did the other two freshmen. 'Dear Mr Minthauser, We shall be so glad if you will come to tea next Sunday at half-past four. Yours sincerely, Muriel Bindloss.'

Muriel Bindloss was presumably the wife of Mr Bindloss, their tutor. . . .

On these Sunday afternoons early in Michaelmas Term between four and half-past four, in bus, on bicycle and on foot, hundreds of undergraduates are moving north to have tea with their tutors.

When Larry arrives, he finds two undergraduates standing on the doorstep.

'Why don't we ring?' he asks.

'We have done, twice. I think the bell is broken.'

'Then why don't we walk straight in?'

'You couldn't very well do that, could you? I mean. . . .'

'Come on.'

Larry opens the door and, once in the hall, shouts, 'Anybody at home?'

The other two, who are English, keep their distance, shocked by such un-English behaviour.

A small boy opens a door and comes into the hall. His face needs washing.

'Hullo,' he says.

'Hullo.'

'My rabbit has just died,' the child says.

'Well, if that isn't a shame.'

'I gave it salad-dressing on its lettuce, like we have. Daddy says that was probably what killed it. I ate some too, and it made me sick. My sick was all green.'

'What a shame.'

'I don't mind, really. It was a very silly rabbit, because it couldn't have little rabbits. Like our cat – but *she's* had an operation. What have you come for?'

'We've been asked to tea.'

'Oh, you'd better go in there – unless you'd rather come and see my trains.'

'I think we'd better go in.'

The room is in some confusion. A child is sitting in a high chair, tearing some galley-proofs to pieces. On their hands and knees on the floor are two men and two women.

One of the women says, 'I'm sure it's not on the floor. I know there were nine beads, and now there are only eight. The child *must* have swallowed it. I don't suppose it matters.'

They rise to their feet.

'Oh, hullo,' Mr Bindloss says, 'Muriel, let me introduce Mr . . .'

'Minthauser,' Larry says, to help out. 'Call me Larry.'

'Of course, and . . .'

'Mr Harrison.'

'Mr Jukes.'

'Of course.'

Larry can hardly take his eyes off his hostess. If she had a bath and went to a hairdresser and if somebody explained to her that brown is a colour which suits few women and which suits her least of all, she would be an extremely attractive woman.

'And this,' she says, 'is my sister and her husband.'

'Oh God,' Mr Bindloss says. 'Are those my proofs?'

They are – or were.

'Never mind, dear,' his wife says, 'I will see if I can stick them together afterwards. Harcourt, have you buried that filthy rabbit?'

'No,' the small boy says. 'I've built a bonfire and I'm going to *burn* it. I want daddy to get a prayer-book and read some prayers.'

'I suppose,' Mrs Bindloss says, 'that we ought to have tea. It's probably cold by now.'

Dacre Balsdon, *Oxford Life*, 1957

THE NON-ALCOHOLIC DRINK

*In the first of these examples of a guest receiving an un-
usually disconcerting reception, Evelyn Waugh's character,
Adam Symes, has made the journey out of London to
Doubting Hall to have lunch with the father of Nina
Blount, the girl he wants to marry.*

"Ere y'are,' said the driver.

Adam paid him and went up the steps to the front
door. He rang the bell and waited. Nothing happened.
Presently he rang again. At this moment the door
opened.

'Don't ring twice,' said a very angry old man. 'What
do you want?'

'Is Mr Blount in?'

'There's no Mr Blount here. This is Colonel Blount's
house.'

'I'm sorry. I think the Colonel is expecting me to
luncheon.'

'Nonsense. I'm Colonel Blount,' and he shut the door.

The Ford had disappeared. It was still raining hard.
Adam rang again.

'Yes,' said Colonel Blount, appearing instantly.

'I wonder if you'd let me telephone to the station for
a taxi?'

'Not on the telephone. It's raining. Why don't you

come in? It's absurd to walk to the station in this. Have you come about the vacuum cleaner?'

'No.'

'Funny, I've been expecting a man all the morning to show me a vacuum cleaner. Come in, do. Won't you stay to luncheon?'

'I should love to.'

'Splendid. I get very little company nowadays. You must forgive me for opening the door to you myself. My butler is in bed to-day. He suffers terribly in his feet when it is wet. Both my footmen were killed in the war. Put your hat and coat here. I hope you haven't got wet. I'm sorry you didn't bring the vacuum cleaner, but never mind. How are you?' he said, suddenly holding out his hand.

They shook hands and Colonel Blount led the way down a long corridor, lined with marble busts on yellow marble pedestals, to a large room full of furniture, with a fire burning in a fine rococo fireplace. There was a large leather-topped walnut writing-table under a window opening on to a terrace. Colonel Blount picked up a telegram and read it.

'I'd quite forgotten,' he said in some confusion. 'I'm afraid you'll think me very discourteous, but it is, after all, impossible for me to ask you to luncheon. I have a guest coming on very intimate family business. You understand, don't you? To tell you the truth, it's some young rascal who wants to marry my daughter. I must see him alone to discuss settlements.'

'Well, I want to marry your daughter, too,' said Adam.

'What an extraordinary coincidence. Are you sure you do?'

'Perhaps the telegram may be about me. What does it say?'

' "*Engaged to marry Adam Symes. Expect him lunch-*

eon. Nina." Are you Adam Symes?'

'Yes.'

'My dear boy, why didn't you say so before, instead of going on about a vacuum cleaner? How are you?'

Evelyn Waugh, *Vile Bodies*, 1930

Winnie-the-Pooh goes visiting.

'If I know anything about anything, that hole means Rabbit,' he said, 'and Rabbit means Company,' he said, 'and Company means Food and Listening-to-Me-Humming and such like. *Rum-tum-tum-tiddle-um.*'

So he bent down, put his head into the hole, and called out:

'Is anybody at home?'

There was a sudden scuffling noise from inside the hole, and then silence.

'What I said was, "Is anybody at home?" ' called out Pooh very loudly.

'No!' said a voice; and then added, 'You needn't shout so loud. I heard you quite well the first time.'

'Bother!' said Pooh. 'Isn't there anybody here at all?'

'Nobody.'

Winnie-the-Pooh took his head out of the hole, and thought for a little, and he thought to himself, 'There must be somebody there, because somebody must have *said* "Nobody." ' So he put his head back in the hole, and said:

'Hallo, Rabbit, isn't that you?'

'No,' said Rabbit, in a different sort of voice this time.

'But isn't that Rabbit's voice?'

'I don't *think* so,' said Rabbit. 'It isn't *meant* to be.'

'Oh!' said Pooh.

He took his head out of the hole, and had another think, and then he put it back, and said:

'Well, could you very kindly tell me where Rabbit is?'

'He has gone to see his friend Pooh Bear, who is a great friend of his.'

'But this *is* Me!' said Bear, very much surprised.

'What sort of Me?'

'Pooh Bear.'

'Are you sure?' said Rabbit, still more surprised.

'Quite, quite sure,' said Pooh.

'Oh, well, then, come in.'

A. A. Milne, *Winnie-the-Pooh*, 1926

The following passage, showing the effects of some inspired stage-management on a guest's arrival, is from England Their England, *and illustrates what Stephen Potter called Important Person Play. (See page 35.) The hero of the book, Donald Cameron, is an innocent Scot making the acquaintance of English life between the wars. He has been invited by the leading society hostess, Lady Ormerode, to a weekend party at Ormerode Towers, and as he puzzles in his lodgings over what to pack, Mr Huggins, great grandson of the Mayor of Bolton, arrives to drink a quantity of wine at ten in the morning, and offer advice.*

'Cameron, be guided by me. The crux of the week-end is the servant. Do you follow me?'

'N-no. Not quite.'

'I should have thought I had made my explanation fool-proof,' said Mr Huggins severely, 'but apparently I haven't. Listen carefully. Get at the rich man's servant before he gets at you. Treat 'em rough and they're lovely. Treat 'em humble and they're hell.' ...

'But you haven't told me what clothes to take,' cried Donald in despair, shaking him vigorously. Mr Huggins woke up and struggled uncertainly to his feet. ...

'Hullo! what's all this? My dear chap! Why didn't you ask me before? Clothes! that's the problem. And

I'll give you the solution. Take all the clothes you've got. The more the better. Take one suitcase; the butler sneers, the footmen giggle, the under house-parlour-maids have hysterics. Take fifty and they'll treat you like the Duke of Westminster.'

'But I've only got two small suitcases,' objected Donald plaintively. 'I brought all the rest of my things from Scotland in a trunk and a valise. Besides, some of my things are so old that I couldn't possibly take them.'

Mr Huggins was seized with demoniac energy. He drained off Donald's glass. He routed out the two small suitcases. He rushed out of the house and roared at a passing taxi so that the windows shook, and rushed back in ten minutes with twelve second-hand suitcases that he had bought at a shop in Sloane Square, and a bundle of enormous labels and a pot of red paint, and started to pack all Donald's belongings into them. Donald's protests were overridden tempestuously. For instance, when he pleaded almost tearfully, 'I can't take a pair of grey flannels with a hole in the knee,' the invincible Mr Huggins whipped out a pair of scissors and instantly converted the trousers into shorts, exclaiming as he did so, 'There you are! Shorts for otter-hunting. Put them in the otter-hunting suitcase.'

An old football outfit was packed with the description, 'Beagling kit'. A battered bowler hat, two frayed dressing-gowns, a broken umbrella, odd shoes, books, newspapers, bits of rope, photographs and pictures, were all crammed into another suitcase and labelled by Mr Huggins 'Amateur Theatricals', and one entire suitcase was filled with old newspapers and solemnly corded up and sealed and labelled, in huge scarlet letters, 'Dispatches; Secret'. It was useless for Donald to protest, for Mr Huggins paid no attention to him whatsoever. Nor was it possible to escape from this appalling accumulation of luggage by depositing it in the cloakroom at the station, for Mr Huggins insisted upon accompanying him to the station himself, and caused poor Donald agonies of embarrassment and confusion by engaging two porters to carry the Secret Dispatches, in addition to two others for the remaining packages, and by addressing Donald deferentially but loudly, all the time as 'Excellency'. Nor were Donald's apprehensions allayed by the last mysterious whispered words of his self-appointed and unwanted ally as the train steamed out, 'I'll fix that bloody butler. Trust me.'

A Rolls-Royce met the train at Godalming, and Donald felt like bursting into tears as suitcase after suitcase emerged from the station. He was too miserable to notice the subtle increase of deference with which each piece of luggage was greeted by the chauffeur and footman. The station-master himself attended with his own hands to the Secret Dispatches, murmuring discreetly in Donald's ear, 'I was warned by telephone, my lord, from our Head Office.' He was charmed by Donald's unassuming manner and his half-crown.

Just before it reached the front door of Ormerode Towers, the Rolls-Royce loosed several melodious toots upon the summery air, obviously a prearranged signal, and half a dozen flunkeys came tumbling down the broad steps followed, with great majesty, by the butler. As Donald disentangled himself from the huge fur rug with which the chauffeur had insisted upon enveloping him, and scrambled out of the mammoth automobile, the butler sidled up to him respectfully and whispered in his ear, 'The Secretary of the French Foreign Ministry rang up, sir, and Budapest has also been on the line. Budapest is to telephone again, sir.'

Donald was completely staggered by this information until he reflected that this must be Mr Huggins' amiable method of 'fixing that bloody butler'.

A. G. Macdonnell, *England Their England*, 1930

Here are two more examples of the servants' response to a guest's luggage. The first story is told by John Aubrey (1626–97) in his life of Thomas Allen, the sixteenth-century Oxford mathematician.

One time being at Hom Lacy in Herefordshire, at Mr John Scudamore's (grandfather to the Lord Scudamor) he happened to leave his Watch in the Chamber windowe. (Watches were then rarities.) The maydes came in to make the Bed, and hearing a thing in a case cry *Tick, Tick, Tick,* presently concluded that that was his Devill, and tooke it by the String with the tongues [tongs], and threw it out of the windowe into the Mote (to drowne the Devill). It so happened that the string hung on a sprig of an elder that grew out of the Mote, and this confirmed them that 'twas the Devill. So the good old Gentleman gott his Watch again.

John Aubrey, *Brief Lives*

I know of one man who travelled about a bit and kept – in pre-pill days – a supply of contraceptives in his luggage, just in case. He was a Canadian and was horrified on his first experience of the English country-house weekend to arrive in his bedroom to dress for dinner and find three little packets neatly arranged in a row on his dressing table.

An experience of my own was less mortifying, though it must have puzzled the housemaid much more. In the course of a journey between London and Oxford during the war, I stayed a night with friends near Henley, carrying in my suitcase an old, very sharp ham knife with an eighteen-inch blade, which I was taking from my London home to a temporary home in Oxford, and had forgotten to pack with my other belongings when I first moved there.

When I went to my bedroom I found the knife prominently laid out on the dressing table. I have always wanted to know what the housemaid can have thought I travelled with lethal ham knives for, and particularly why – as far as she was concerned – I should have brought it for a one-night stay in Henley.

Spike Hughes, *The Art of Coarse Entertaining*, 1972

THE TWELVE-MILE WALK

Perfect & Imperfect Guests

THE PERFECT GUEST

> She answered by return of post
> The invitation of her host.
> She caught the train she said she would
> And changed at junctions as she should.
> She brought a light and smallish box
> And keys belonging to the locks.
> Food, strange and rare, she did not beg,
> But ate the homely scrambled egg.
> When offered lukewarm tea she drank it.
> She did not crave an extra blanket,
> Nor extra pillows for her head:
> She seemed to like the spare-room bed.
> She never came downstairs till ten,
> She brought her own self-filling pen,
> Nor once by look or word of blame
> Exposed her host to open shame.
> She left no little things behind,
> Excepting . . . loving thoughts and kind.
>
> Rose Henniker Heaton, in *The Perfect Hostess*, 1931

The guest's ability to make himself scarce, whether simply by staying in his bedroom, or by being more actively independent, has always been valued as highly as his entertaining talk.

I came up here yesterday with dear little Dr Oliver Wendell Holmes. He is the most charming guest, like inviting up a delightful elderly bird, that sings whenever you ask it to. He is rather fragile, but has the most delightful readiness in going to bed – has been there twice already to-day – before dinner.

Sir Edmund Gosse, letter to Hamo Thorneycroft, 1886

It is very pleasant here just now. The Harrowboys are staying here and have brought Mr Luttrel and Monsieur de Puysegur. Mr Luttrel is a great walker, a great reader, and passionately fond of music. This makes him independent half the day and easily amused the other, and at dinner it is difficult to be more entertaining. Puysegur is brilliant and witty to the greatest degree, but he has no other resource.

Harriet, Countess of Granville, letter to Lady Morpeth, 1811

Of all the pages of advice to intending perfect guests this, addressed to 1920s American society, or would-be society, is the most demanding. On the subject of loyalty to your host simply because he is your host, compare Katherine Whitehorn advising the 1960s, and Thackeray deflating the 1840s.

Courtesy demands that you, when you are a guest, shall show neither annoyance nor disappointment – no matter what happens. Before you can hope to become even a passable guest, let alone a perfect one, you must learn as it were not to notice if hot soup is poured down your back. If you neither understand nor care for dogs or children, and both insist on climbing all over you, you must seemingly like it; just as you must be amiable and polite to your fellow guests, even though they be of all the people on earth the most detestable to you. You must with the very best dissimulation at your command, appear to find the food delicious though they offer you all of the viands that are especially distasteful to your palate, or antagonistic to your digestion. You must disguise your hatred of red ants and scrambled food, if everyone else is bent on a picnic. You must pretend that six is a perfect dinner hour though you never dine before eight, or, on the contrary, you must wait until eight-thirty or nine with stoical fortitude, though your dinner hour is six and by seven your chest seems securely pinned to your spine.

If you go for a drive, and it pours, and there is no top to the carriage or car, and you are soaked to the skin and chilled to the marrow so that your teeth chatter, your lips must smile and you must appear to enjoy the refreshing coolness.

If you go to stay in a small house in the country, and they give you a bed full of lumps in a room of mosquitoes and flies, in a chamber over that of a crying baby, under the eaves with a temperature of over a hundred, you *can* the next morning walk to the village, and send yourself a telegram and leave! But though you feel starved, exhausted, wilted, and are mosquito bitten until you resemble a well-developed case of chickenpox or measles, by not so much as a facial muscle must you let the family know that your comfort lacked anything that your happiest imagination could picture – nor must you confide in any one afterwards (having broken bread in the house) how desperately wretched you were.

Emily Post, *Etiquette in Society, in Business, in Politics and at Home*, 1922

THE JOLLY TUNES

[23]

It is still not considered a good social opening to start 'I think our hostess is a louse'.

Katharine Whitehorn, *Whitehorn's Social Survival*, 1968

In England Dinner-giving Snobs occupy a very important place in society, and the task of describing them is tremendous. There was a time in my life when the consciousness of having eaten a man's salt rendered me dumb regarding his demerits, and I thought it a wicked act and a breach of hospitality to speak ill of him.

But why should a saddle of mutton blind you, or a turbot and lobster sauce shut your mouth for ever? With advancing age, men see their duties more clearly. I am not to be hoodwinked any longer by a slice of venison, be it ever so fat; and as for being dumb on account of turbot and lobster sauce – of course I am; good manners ordain that I should be so, until I have swallowed the compound – but not afterwards: directly the victuals are discussed, and John takes away the plate my tongue begins to wag. Does not yours, if you have a pleasant neighbour? – a lovely creature, say, of some five-and-thirty, whose daughters have not yet quite come out – they are the best talkers . . . .Suppose you sit next to one of these, how pleasant it is, in the intervals of the banquet, actually to abuse the victuals and the giver of the entertainment!

William Makepeace Thackeray, *A Book of Snobs*, 1847

Dr Johnson, whose opinions on hospitality included 'A man who stays a week with another makes him a slave for a week', was as uninhibited as Thackeray. Here is Boswell on the risks run by anyone who invited Johnson to dine, followed by a demonstration of how to unnerve your host.

He used to descant critically on the dishes which had been at table where he had dined or supped, and to recollect very minutely what he had liked . . . He about the same time was so much displeased with the performances of a nobleman's French cook, that he exclaimed with vehemence, 'I'd throw such a rascal into the river'; and he then proceeded to alarm a lady at whose house he was to sup, by the following manifesto of his skill: 'I, Madam, who live at a variety of good tables, am a much better judge of cookery, than any person who has a very tolerable cook, but lives much at home; for his palate is gradually adapted to the taste of his cook; whereas, Madam, in trying by a wider range, I can more exquisitely judge.' When invited to dine, even with an intimate friend, he was not pleased if something better than a plain dinner was not prepared for him. I have heard him say on such an occasion, 'This was a good dinner enough to be sure; but it was not a dinner to *ask* a man to.'

James Boswell, *Life of Samuel Johnson*, 1791

There is nothing whatever to be said for a dish called suki-aki. Only once before have I ever essayed it, and that was with the great Molly Picon herself. We had been invited by the producer of a play called *Majority of One* which we were then rehearsing, to a genuine Japanese dinner. The ceremony took place in a house in Golders Green, a remote suburb of my capital. Half way through the banquet, when we had sampled the raw fish and other beastliness, Miss Picon was asked what she would like next. 'A doctor,' she told her host.

Robert Morley, *A Musing Morley*, 1974

Gladstone's remarks at table achieved the remarkable feat of inspiring terror in (the admittedly young) Bertrand Russell.

I was alarmed by so formidable a social occasion [the first meal at a Cambridge entrance examination], but less alarmed than I had been a few months earlier when I was left *tête-à-tête* with Mr Gladstone. He came to

[25]

stay at Pembroke Lodge, and nobody was asked to meet him. As I was the only male in the household, he and I were left alone together at the dinner table after the ladies retired. He made only one remark: 'This is very good port they have given me, but why have they given it me in a claret glass?' I did not know the answer, and wished the earth would swallow me up. Since then I have never again felt the full agony of terror.

Bertrand Russell, *Autobiography*, 1967

Like Johnson, the poet W. H. Auden often felt no obligation to say the right thing about the hospitality he was receiving, or indeed to apologize for his own sins. After once making a long cigarette burn on a host's grand piano he said nothing but 'It won't affect the tone'. As an overnight guest he had further eccentricities.

He rose virtually at dawn, a time of day he found good for working, and once up he talked so loudly that he could not be ignored. At meals he shovelled enormous quantities of food into his mouth with no regard for his neighbours' needs. He usually paid no attention to what he was eating – he claimed to have 'the digestion of a horse' – but he could sometimes have unexpected fads. When he was staying with Stephen Spender's family and the dish-cover was lifted at lunch, he exclaimed in tones of severe condemnation, like those of a judge passing sentence: '*Boiled ham!*'.... He was sometimes discovered in the middle of the night raiding the larder for cold potatoes or other left-overs – 'I just wanted to see if that beef was still there', he explained on one such occasion. He invariably piled a huge weight of bedclothes on his bed: blankets, eiderdowns, bedspreads, anything that would make it heavy. If there were not enough of these he would appropriate anything else he could find. At the Fishers' he put the bedroom carpet on his bed. Staying with another

[26]

family, he took down the bedroom curtains and used these as extra blankets. Another time it was the stair-carpet. Once he was discovered in the morning sleeping beneath (among other things) a large framed picture.

Humphrey Carpenter, *W. H. Auden, a biography,* 1981

The guest who is really no trouble at all, content with everything his host provides, is the rarity. Commoner are guests who pretend to be easy, or let their relatives promote that image for them, in advance of a visit. In this letter, King Louis Philippe's daughter Louise prepares Queen Victoria for the King's visit to England.

My dearly beloved Victoria, – ... I have not much to say about my father's *lodging habits* and *likings.* My father is one of the beings *most easy* to *please, satisfy,* and to *accommodate.* His eventful life has used him to everything, and makes any kind of arrangements accep-table to him; there is only *one thing* which he *cannot easily do,* it is to be *ready very early.* He means not-withstanding to try to come to your breakfast, but you *must insist upon his not doing it.* It would disturb him in all his habits, and be bad for him, as he would cer-tainly eat, a thing he is not used to do in the morning. He generally takes hardly what may be called a *break-fast,* and eats *only twice* in the day. It would be also *much better* for him if he only appeared to luncheon and dinner, and if you kindly dispensed him altogether of the breakfast. You must not tell him that I wrote you *this,* but you must manage it with Montpensier, and kindly order for him a bowl of *chicken broth.* It is the only thing he takes generally in the morning, and between his meals. ... About his *rooms,* a hard bed and a large table for his papers are the only things he re-quires. He generally sleeps on a horse-hair mattress with a plank of wood under it: but *any kind* of bed will do, if it is not *too soft.* His liking will be to be entirely at *your commands* and to do *all you like*. You know he can take a great deal of exercise, and *everything* will *interest* and *delight* him, to see, as to do: this is not a compliment, but a *mere fact*. His only wish is, that you should not go out of your way for him, and change your habits on his account.

Louise, Queen of the Belgians, letter to Queen Victoria, 1844

Perhaps a host can be most certain of being properly appreciated, without complaints, when his guests are the professional variety, who cadge meals to survive. Such a guest was Miss Lyse, whom M. F. K. Fisher encountered when living for a while in Dijon with her husband.

She came often to eat with us, too, and I don't think she ever looked once at us. If she did, we were simply a part of all the sixty or so years of people who had fed her. She was charming to us; she sang for her supper, as life had taught her to, and she ate with the same ferocious voracity of any little bird while she kept us entertained ... For years now, Miss Lyse had been cadging meals. She did it charmingly, amusingly. ...

I don't know how she ate so much at one time. It was the result of years of practice, surely, years of not knowing just when another good meal would come her way. She was like a squirrel, with hidden pouches for the future ...

I tried sometimes to see if I could stump her; I would make a bowl of two whole kilos of Belgian endive, cut into chunks and mixed with marinated green beans and sweet red peppers and chives. There would be a big casserole of fish and mushrooms and such in cream. I'd buy rich tarts at Michelin's.

Halfway through the meal Al and I would lie back in our chairs, listening and watching in a kind of daze. Miss Lyse was like something in a Disney film – nibble bite chew nibble nibble – through everything on the table, until it would not have surprised us at all to have her start conversationally, daintily, with a flick of her bright dark eyes and a quirk of her white head, on the plates themselves and then the books, right down the mantelpiece, Shakespeare, Confucius, *Claudine à l'Ecole, les Croix de Bois, The Methodist Faun,* – nibble nibble crunch.

'That was so delicious, my dear,' she would say at the end, wiping her mouth nicely and getting up with a brisk bob. 'You are most kind to an old lady. And now I must thank you and be off. The Countess Malinet de Rinche is in from the country and I am having tea with her. This was *such* a nice little lunch together! Shall we say for the same day next week? Then I can tell you all about the dear Countess! Her sons! *Mon Dieu!*'

And Miss Lyse would give me a dry sweet-smelling peck on both cheeks and be out of the door before we could even get to our feet.

Would she really have tea with the unknown Countess What's-her-name, whose sons were less interesting than dead sea-fruit to us? Would she eat again until we next saw her? Did she really have *sous* enough for bread? We never knew.

M. F. K. Fisher, *The Art of Eating,* 1963

The careful cadger of hospitality, who offers talk and entertainment as payment, is never as exasperating as the truly uninvited guest, or the one who makes a habit of mistaking the day. Violet Trefusis, self-styled daughter of Edward VII and literary celebrity, was the bane of the lives of her Paris friends such as Nancy Mitford.

We had a rhyme:

> Violet Trefusis
> Never refuses
> But often confuses.

'I've got a luncheon party today. Violet arrived for it yesterday,' Nancy told Heywood Hill. 'I was eating a little bit of fish. I said you MUST go away but she tottered to the table, scooped up all the fish and all the potatoes, left half and threw cigarette ash over it. I could have KILLED her.'

Harold Acton, *Nancy Mitford, A Memoir*, 1975

Beatrix Potter's houseproud Mrs Tittlemouse is the type of the polite but unwilling hostess, invaded first by insects and then by Mr Jackson the toad, all 'without any invitation'.

Mrs Tittlemouse began to pull out the moss. Three or four other bees put their heads out, and buzzed fiercely.

'I am not in the habit of letting lodgings; this is an intrusion!' said Mrs Tittlemouse. 'I will have them turned out – '

'Buzz! Buzz! Buzz!'

'I wonder who would help me? . . . I will not have Mr Jackson; he never wipes his feet.' Mrs Tittlemouse decided to leave the bees till after dinner.

When she got back to the parlour, she heard someone coughing in a fat voice; and there sat Mr Jackson himself! He was sitting all over a small rocking-chair, twiddling his thumbs and smiling, with his feet on the fender. He lived in a drain below the hedge, on a very dirty wet ditch.

'How do you do, Mr Jackson? Deary me, you have got very wet!'

'Thank you, thank you, Mrs Tittlemouse! I'll sit awhile and dry myself,' said Mr Jackson.

He sat and smiled, and the water dripped off his coat tails. Mrs Tittlemouse went round with a mop.

He sat such a while that he had to be asked if he would take some dinner.

Beatrix Potter, *The Tale of Mrs Tittlemouse*, 1910

Mr Pooter, the hero of Diary of a Nobody, *is similarly nonplussed by the self-confidence and sheer bulk of an uninvited guest. Mr Burwin-Fosselton, a friend of Pooter's ne'er-do-well son Lupin, has promised his imitation of Irving, and Pooter's friends Cummings and Gowing have been invited to make up an audience.*

NOVEMBER 23. In the evening, Cummings came early. Gowing came a little later and brought, without asking permission, a fat and, I think, very vulgar-looking man named Padge, who appeared to be all moustache. Gowing never attempted any apology to either of us, but said Padge wanted to see the Irving business, to which Padge said: 'That's right', and that is about all he *did* say during the entire evening. Lupin came in and seemed in much better spirits. He had prepared a bit of a surprise. Mr Burwin-Fosselton had come in with him, but had gone upstairs to get ready. In half-an-hour Lupin retired from the parlour, and returning in a few minutes, announced 'Mr Henry Irving'.

I must say we were all astounded. I never saw such a resemblance. It was astonishing. The only person who did not appear interested was the man Padge, who had got the best armchair, and was puffing away at a foul pipe into the fireplace.

After supper, Mr Burwin-Fosselton got a little too boisterous over his Irving imitation, and suddenly seizing Gowing by the collar of his coat, dug his thumb-nail, accidentally of course, into Gowing's neck and took a piece of flesh out. Gowing was rightly annoyed, but that man Padge, who having declined our modest supper in order that he should not lose his comfortable chair, burst into an uncontrollable fit of laughter at the little misadventure. I was so annoyed at the conduct of Padge, I said: 'I suppose you would have laughed if he had poked Mr Gowing's eye out?' to which Padge replied: 'That's right', and laughed more than ever. I think perhaps the greatest surprise was when we broke up, for Mr Burwin-Fosselton said: 'Good night, Mr Pooter. I'm glad you like the imitation. I'll bring *the other make-up tomorrow night.*'

NOVEMBER 24 ... Dear old Cummings came in the evening; but Gowing sent round a little note saying he hoped I would excuse his not turning up, which rather amused me. He added that his neck was still painful. Of course, Burwin-Fosselton came, but Lupin never turned up, and imagine my utter disgust when that man Padge actually came again, and not even accompanied by Gowing. I was exasperated, and said: 'Mr Padge, this is a *surprise.*' Dear Carrie, fearing unpleasantness, said: 'Oh, I suppose Mr Padge has only come to see the other Irving make-up.' Mr Padge said: 'That's right', and took the best chair again, from which he never moved the whole evening.

My only consolation is, he takes no supper, so he is not an expensive guest, but I shall speak to Gowing about the matter. ... When they left, I very pointedly said to Mr Burwin-Fosselton and Mr Padge that we should be engaged tomorrow evening.

George and Weedon Grossmith, *Diary of a Nobody,* 1892

THE EARLY RETIREMENT

In a different class is the gatecrashing and hoaxing of which the writer and wit Theodore Hook (1788–1841) is said to have been master. He was once accountant general of Mauritius, but was recalled because of a deficiency of £12,000 in the accounts or, as he called it, 'a disorder in his chest'. His most famous practical joke was the Berners Street hoax of 1809, when he sent out more than 4,000 letters summoning everyone from the Duke of Gloucester to a chimney sweep, to attend the house of a Mrs Tottenham. The street was jammed for a whole day. This is one of the many stories told of him and his circle of friends, followed by another that shows such escapades to have occasionally gone awry.

Two young men are strolling, towards 5 p.m. in the then fashionable neighbourhood of Soho; the one is Terry, the actor – the other, Hook, the actor, for surely he deserves the title. They pass a house, and sniff the viands cooking underground. Hook quietly announces his intention of dining *there*. He enters, is admitted and announced by the servant, mingles with the company, and is quite at home before he is perceived by the host. At last the *dénouement* came; the dinner-giver approached the stranger, and with great politeness asked his name. 'Smith' was, of course, the reply, and reverting to mistakes made by servants in announcing, &c., 'Smith' hurried off into an amusing story, to put his host in good humour.

'But, really, my dear sir,' the host put in, 'I think the mistake on the present occasion does not originate in the source you allude to; I certainly did not anticipate the honour of Mr Smith's company to-day.'

'No, I dare say not. You said *four* in your note, I know, and it is now, I see, a quarter past five; but the fact is, I have been detained in the City, as I was going to explain – '

'Pray,' said the host, 'whom do you suppose you are addressing?'

'Whom? why Mr Thompson, of course, old friend of my father. I have not the pleasure, indeed, of being personally known to you, but having received your kind invitation yesterday,' &c. &c.

'No, sir, my name is not Thompson, but Jones,' in highly indignant accents.

'Jones!' was the well-acted answer: 'why, surely, I cannot have – yes I must – good heaven! I see it all. My *dear* sir, what an unfortunate blunder; wrong house – what must you think of such an intrusion? I am really at a loss for words in which to apologize; you will permit me to retire at present, and to morrow –'

'Pray, don't think of retiring,' rejoined the host, taken with the appearance and manner of the young man. 'Your friend's table must have been cleared long ago, if, as you say, four was the hour named, and I am too happy to be able to offer you a seat at mine.'

Hook's friend, little Tom Hill, of whom it was said that he knew everybody's affairs far better than they did themselves, was famous for examining kitchens about the hour of dinner, and quietly selecting his host according to the odour of the viands. It is of him that the old 'Joe Miller' is told of the 'haunch of venison.' Invited to dinner at one house, he *happens* to glance down into the kitchen of the next, and seeing a tempting haunch of venison on the spit, throws over the inviter, and ingratiates himself with his neighbour, who ends by asking him to stay to dinner. The fare, however, consisted of nothing more luxurious than an Irish stew, and the disappointed guest was informed that he had been 'too cunning by half,' inasmuch as the venison belonged to his original inviter, and had been cooked in the house he was in by kind permission, because the chimney of the owner's kitchen smoked.

Grace and Philip Wharton, *The Wits and Beaux of Society*,
1860

*Gatecrashing would apparently have been even easier at
the most celebrated of all English weekend parties, those
given at Cliveden by Viscount Astor and his American
wife Nancy, the first woman Member of Parliament.
Joyce Grenfell was the daughter of Lady Astor's sister.*

The company was varied and it was not unusual to
meet a duchess, with or without her duke, MPs of all
parties, an international banker, a Christian Science
lecturer, all mixed up with friends from Uncle Waldorf's English youth and my aunt's American girlhood;
and there were younger married couples and, often, a
lonely man or woman whom no one seemed to know
and whose identity was never discovered throughout
the weekend. My mother always believed it would be
possible for an adventurer to stay at Cliveden unde-
tected, because Aunt Nancy would expect he'd been
asked by Uncle Waldorf or *vice versa*.

Joyce Grenfell Requests the Pleasure, 1976

*Stephen Potter's manual of week-endmanship suggests a
gentler, but just as effective, form of deceit: Important
Person Play.*

There is no doubt that basic week-endmanship should
contain some reference to Important Person Play. It
must appear that it is *you* who in mid-week life are the
most important man. I always like to quote here the
plucky ploying of poor Geoffrey Field. On the Friday
evening he always seemed pretty done in. No question
of having to entertain Field, or, indeed, of Field entertaining. He was there for a rest – had to be, got to be,
if he was going to get through next week's work. He
would lie back, legs out, eyes relaxed, arms hanging

straight down on the sides of the chair – content. 'Sh – they won't ring me up because (not a word) nobody knows where I am. Except Bales.'

No one knew who Bales was, and only I knew that he didn't exist, and that in fact Field had been out of a job for nine months. Yet there was a general tendency among the guests actually to wait on Field – tend him. At Liverpool Street on Monday morning Field used to say, 'Taxi? No thanks. The Ministry is sending or is alleged to be sending a car for me.'

When everybody had gone, Field would take a four-penny tube to Ealing Broadway, and play squash on the public courts, or rather knock up by himself.

Stephen Potter, *Lifemanship*, 1950

Lower down the social scale than Cliveden, the fashion for weekend parties coincided with a shortage of servants. Stephen Potter had a ploy for this too.

Let me, to start with, transcribe here a few notes, I believe not unimportant, on the typical Week-endman – based, I should add, on that grand Lifeman with that fine old week-end name, G. Cogg-Willoughby.

What to record? I remember Cogg-Willoughby's first action, coming down to supper – a late cold meal, on the first night – the Friday night. . . . Immediately the meal was over, Cogg-Willoughby would take off his coat, roll up his sleeves, clear the table in a trice, and then, 'Let's get down to it,' he said, and would do all the washing-up, if not part of the drying-up as well, expertly and thoroughly, with a quick swish round even of one or two saucepans, and clean a cup, used at some previous meal with which he had no connection. No need to add that, having planted this good impression in the mind of his hostess, 'Cogg' for the rest of the week-end would lift not one finger in the kitchen or the garden, nor bring in so much as a single log of fire-wood from the shed.

Stephen Potter, *Lifemanship*, 1950

The worst guests remain invited guests, without deceit or pretensions. Here are some of them, described with the awesome candour of two Regency lady letter-writers, followed by Horace Walpole's equally devastating remarks about the majority of his fellow guests.

Miss P. is something of a failure in every way, except in intrinsic goodness; but she was terrified here, and at all times dull, and as nearly ugly as is lawful.

Emily Eden, letter to Miss Villiers, 1821

The Jerseys go tomorrow. ... They both like me as much as they can the person in the whole world who suits them least, and I am sure we feel at moments equal remorse at finding our affections towards each other so cold and dead in the midst of so many efforts and acts of kindness. I would risk my life for them rather than spend a week with them.

Harriet, Countess of Granville, letter to Lady Morpeth, 1817

We have had a spirt of company for the last three days, but they all very kindly walked off yesterday, and as it is wrong to dwell upon past evils, I spare you an account of them.

Emily Eden, letter to the Dowager Lady Buckinghamshire, 1819

Oh! my dear Sir, don't you find that nine parts in ten of the world are of no use but to make you wish your-self with that tenth part! I am so far from growing used to mankind by living amongst them, that my natural ferocity and wildness does but every day grow worse. They tire me, they fatigue me; I don't know what to do with them, I don't know what to say to them; I fling open the windows and fancy I want air; and when I get by myself, I undress myself, and seem to have had people in my pockets, in my plaits and on my shoulders! I indeed find this fatigue worse in the country than in town, because one can avoid it there and has more resources, but it is there too – I fear 'tis growing old – but I literally seem to have murdered a man whose name was ennui, for his ghost is ever before me. They say there is no English word for ennui; I think you may translate it most literally by what is called *entertaining people and doing the honours*. That is, you sit an hour with somebody you don't know and don't care for, talk about the wind and the weather, and ask a thousand foolish questions, which all begin with, *I think you live a good deal in the country*, or *I think you don't love this thing or that*. Oh! 'tis dreadful!

Horace Walpole, letter to John Chute, 1743

The scholarship of Professor Richard Porson of Cambridge (1759–1808) was proverbial. So were the shattered nerves of anyone who entertained him. He was an archetypal absent-minded academic, who 'would forget to eat dinner, though he never forgot a quotation', and once when invited to dine he replied, 'Thank you, no, I dined yesterday.' But he was also famous for his appetite for wine, and for the stamina that made entertaining him a nightmare.

The unfortunate Mr Horne Tooke, for instance, was one of Professor Porson's unhappier hosts, for he was foolish enough to invite the Professor to dine with him on a night that he knew had been preceded by three nights in which the Professor had refused all entreaties on the part of his hosts that he should go home to bed. Mr Tooke thought, therefore, that Professor Porson would relent on this occasion. But the night wore on, and Mr Tooke was worn out, for the Professor became more and more animated, passing from one learned theme to another. . . . Dawn broke, the birds sang, the milkman shouted, the Professor continued his monologue. At last, in mid morning, the exhausted Mr Tooke proclaimed that he had an engagement to meet a friend for breakfast in a coffee-house at Leicester Square. The Professor was delighted, and announced that he would come too. But in the end, Providence came to the rescue of Mr Tooke and, soon after the Professor and he were seated in the coffee-house, the Professor's attention was distracted for an instant, and Mr Tooke, seizing the opportunity, fled as fast as his legs would carry him, nor did he pause for breath until he had reached Richmond Buildings. Having reached this haven of refuge, he barricaded himself in, and ordered his servant not to admit the Professor even if he should attempt to batter down the door. For 'a man', Mr Tooke observed, 'who could sit up four nights successively, could sit up forty'.

Edith Sitwell, *English Eccentrics*, 1933

Of all imperfect guests, one of the most memorably outrageous is Kingsley Amis's Jim Dixon. A young university lecturer, he is invited to a weekend party (with madrigals) at the home of his insufferable professor. After picking a fight with his host's son, Dixon absconds to a pub for the rest of the evening, returns home drunk, makes unwelcome advances to a fellow guest, and before going to bed helps himself to a large quantity of the professor's port. The following morning he awakes with an exceptional hangover.

Dixon was alive again. . . . He reached out for and put on his glasses. At once he saw that something was wrong with the bedclothes immediately before his face.

Endangering his chance of survival, he sat up a little, and what met his bursting eyes roused to a frenzy the timpanist in his head. A large, irregular area of the turned-back part of the sheet was missing; a smaller but still considerable area of the turned-back part of the blanket was missing; an area about the size of the palm of his hand in the main part of the top blanket was missing. Through the three holes, which, appropriately enough, had black borders, he could see a dark brown mark on the second blanket. He ran a finger round a bit of the hole in the sheet, and when he looked at his finger it bore a dark-grey stain. That meant ash: ash meant burning; burning must mean cigarettes. Had this cigarette burnt itself out on the blanket? If not, where was it now? Nowhere on the bed; nor in it. He leaned over the side, gritting his teeth; a sunken brown channel, ending in a fragment of discoloured paper, lay across a light patch in the pattern of a valuable-looking rug. This made him feel very unhappy, a feeling sensibly increased when he looked at the bedside table. This was marked by two black, charred grooves, greyish and shiny in parts, lying at right angles and stopping well short of the ashtray, which held a single used match....

He got out of bed and went into the bathroom. After a minute or two he returned, eating toothpaste and carrying a safety-razor blade. He started carefully cutting round the edges of the burnt areas of the bedclothes with the blade. He didn't know why he did this, but the operation did seem to improve the look of things: the cause of the disaster wasn't so immediately apparent....

He was all ready to slink down to the phone when, returning to the bedroom, he again surveyed the mutilated bedclothes. They looked in some way unsatisfactory; he couldn't have said how. He went and locked the outer bathroom door, picked up the razor-blade, and began again on the circumferences of the holes. This time he made jagged cuts into the material, little inlets from the great missing areas. Some pieces he almost severed. Finally he held the blade at right angles and ran it quickly round the holes, roughening them up. He stood back from his work and decided the effect was perceptibly better. The disaster now seemed much less obviously the work of man and might, for a few seconds, be put down to some fulminant dry-rot or the ravages of a colony of moths. He turned the rug round so that the shaven burn, without being actually hidden by a nearby chair, was none the less not far from it. He was considering taking the bedside table downstairs and later throwing it out of the bus on his journey back when a familiar voice came into aural range. ...

Kingsley Amis, *Lucky Jim*, 1954

THE GUEST CHAMBER

THE PERFECT PEST

She merely sent a wire to say
That she was coming down to stay.
She brought a maid of minxsome look
Who promptly quarrelled with the cook.
She smoked, and dropped with ruthless hand
Hot ashes on the Steinway grand.
She strode across the parquet floors
With hobnailed boots from out of doors.
She said the water wasn't hot,
And Jane gave notice on the spot.
She snubbed the wealthy dull relations
From whom my wife had expectations.
She kept her bell in constant peals,
She never was in time for meals.
And when at last with joyful heart
We thrust her in the luggage cart,
In half an hour she came again,
And said . . . 'My dear, I've missed the train!'

Adrian Porter, in *The Perfect Hostess*, 1931

Perfect & Imperfect Hosts

The hospitality of the Middle East is so renowned that this selection of fine hosts begins with Persian hospitality at the end of the nineteenth century. The writer of the description is Gertrude Bell (1868–1926) who travelled alone through Arabia, worked in the British intelligence service during the First World War, and became influential in Middle East affairs.

I never knew what desert was till I came here; it is a very wonderful thing to see; and suddenly in the middle of it all, out of nothing, out of a little cold water, springs up a garden. . . . Here sits the enchanted prince, solemn, dignified, clothed in long robes. He comes down to meet you as you enter, his house is yours, his garden is yours, better still his tea and fruit are yours, so are his kalyans (but I think kalyans are a horrid form of smoke, they taste to me of charcoal and paint and nothing else). By the grace of God your slave hopes that the health of your nobility is well? It is very well out of his great kindness. Will your magnificence carry itself on to this cushion? Your magnificence sits down and spends ten minutes in bandying florid compliments through an interpreter while ices are served and coffee, after which you ride home refreshed, charmed, and with many blessings on your fortunate head. And all the time your host was probably a perfect stranger into whose privacy you had forced yourself in this unblushing way. Ah, we have no hospitality in the west and no manners.

Gertrude Bell, letter to Horace Marshall, 1892

The Middle East has had the advantage of religions with specific rules of hospitality, as well as a climate in which travellers can often only survive if offered food, drink, and shelter by strangers. But for all the vehemence of the code that the stranger who has accepted hospitality is sacred, there were spectacular breaches. Jael, for instance, in the Old Testament, gives Sisera milk to drink and a rug to lie under in her tent, and then drives a tent-peg into his skull. And Mehemet Ali, the Moslem Pasha of Egypt, when he wanted to get rid of the powerful Mamelukes, simply invited them to the citadel, served them with coffee, and then had them massacred.

Max Beerbohm sees Old Wardle, Dickens's character in Pickwick Papers, *as the image of the perfect English host. But then he analyses his motives.*

In life or literature there has been no better host than Old Wardle. Appalling though he would have been as a guest in club or restaurant, it is hardly less painful to think of him as a host there. At Dingley Dell, with an ample gesture, he made you free of all that was his. He could not have given you a club or a restaurant. Nor, when you come to think of it, did he give you Dingley Dell. The place remained his. None knew better than Old Wardle that this was so. Hospitality, as we have agreed, is not one of the most deep-rooted instincts in man, whereas the sense of possession certainly is. Not even Old Wardle was a communist. 'This', you may be sure he said to himself, 'is *my* roof, these are *my* horses, that's a picture of *my* dear old grandfather.' And 'This', he would say to us, 'is *my* roof: sleep soundly under it. These are *my* horses: ride them. That's a portrait of *my* dear old grandfather: have a good look at it.' But he did not ask us to walk off with any of these things. Not even what he actually did give us would he regard as having passed out of his possession. 'That', he would muse if we were torpid after dinner, 'is *my* roast beef', and 'That', if we staggered on the way to bed, 'is *my* cold milk punch'. 'But surely,' you interrupt me, 'to give and then not feel that one has given is the very best of all ways of giving.' I agree. I hope you didn't think I was trying to disparage Old Wardle. I was merely keeping my promise to point out that from among the motives of even the best hosts pride and egoism are not absent.

Hosts and Guests, 1920

Pride certainly tinges the pleasure that Samuel Pepys got from entertaining, but that is no reason for him to seem a less delightful host. Every March he gave a dinner to celebrate the successful removal of a stone from his kidney, and whenever possible his guests included the woman in whose house the operation had been performed, Madam Turner. 'The' is Theophila Turner.

Up earely – this being, by God's great blessing, the fourth solemne day of my cutting for the stone this day four year. And am by God's mercy in very good health, and like to do well, the Lord's name be praised for it. . . . At noon came my good guest Madam Turner, The, and Cosen Norton, and a gentleman, one Mr Lewin of the King's life-guard. . . . I had a pretty dinner for them – *viz*: a brace of stewed Carps, six roasted chicken, and a Jowle of salmon hot, for the first course – a Tanzy and two neats' tongues and cheese the second. And were very merry all the afternoon, talking and singing and piping on the Flagelette. In the evening they went with great pleasure away. . .

Samuel Pepys, *Diary*, 26 March 1662

Before turning to imperfect hosts, the story of poor would-be-perfect Sir Christopher Hatton must be told. He was Lord Chancellor to Queen Elizabeth I and built a huge house at Holdenby especially to entertain the Queen and her retinue – something like 150 people all told. He expected her to visit him regularly, as she did Lord Burghley in his equally large new house. Hatton put himself heavily into debt to build a house with two complete courtyards, to provide separate accommodation for the Queen's household; as a bachelor he could never use all this himself. The Queen never came. Hatton died, leaving Holdenby to a nephew who could not afford it, and not long afterwards the house was demolished.

The first of the host's sins is dullness. The characteristics of a host, or his surroundings, that make a visit boring are notoriously hard to define. They are also found among the highest in the land.

I shall continue to think a visit to Chatsworth a very great trouble. You are probably right in thinking the Duke takes pleasure in making people do what they don't like, and that accounts for his asking me so often. We have now made a rule to accept one invitation out of two. We go there with the best dispositions, wishing to be amused, liking the people we meet there, loyal and well affected to the King of the Peak himself, supported by the knowledge that in the eyes of the neighbourhood we are covering ourselves with glory by frequenting the *great house*; but with all these helps we have never been able to stay above two days there without finding change of air absolutely necessary, – never could turn the corner of the third day. . . . We were obliged to pretend that some christening, or a grand funeral, or some pressing case of wedding (in this country it is sometimes expedient to hurry the performance of the marriage ceremony) required Robert's immediate return home, and so we departed yawning. It is odd it should be so dull. The G. Lambs are both pleasant, and so is Mr Foster and Mrs Cavendish and a great many of the

habitués of Chatsworth; and though I have not yet
attained the real Derbyshire feeling which would bring
tears of admiration into my eyes whenever the Duke
observed that it was a fine day, yet I think him pleasant,
and like him very much, and can make him hear without
any difficulty, and he is very hospitable and wishes us
to bring all our friends and relations there, if that would
do us any good. But we happen to be *pleasanter* at home.

Emily Eden, letter to Miss Villers, 1825

The party was certainly very dull, as were all such dinners at Guestwick Manor. There are houses which, in
their everyday course, are not conducted by any means
in a sad or unsatisfactory manner, – in which life, as a
rule, runs along merrily enough; but which cannot give
a dinner-party; or, I might rather say, should never
allow themselves to be allured into the attempt. The
owners of such houses are generally themselves quite
aware of the fact, and dread the dinner which they
resolved to give quite as much as it is dreaded by their
friends. They know that they prepare for their guests an
evening of misery, and for themselves certain long hours
of purgatory which are hardly to be endured. But they
will do it. Why that long table, and all those super-
numerary glasses and knives and forks, if they are never
to be used? That argument produces all this misery;
that and others cognate to it. On the present occasion,
no doubt, there were excuses to be made. The squire
and his niece had been invited on special cause, and
their presence would have been well enough. The
doctor added in would have done no harm. It was goodnatured, too, that invitation given to Mrs Eames and
her daughter. The error lay in the parson and his wife.
There was no necessity for their being there, nor had
they any ground on which to stand, except the party-
giving ground. Mr and Mrs Boyce made the dinner-

party, and destroyed the social circle. Lady Julia knew that she had been wrong as soon as she had sent out the note.

Nothing was said on that evening which has any bearing on our story. Nothing, indeed, was said which had any bearing on anything. The earl's professed object had been to bring the squire and young Eames together; but people are never brought together on such melancholy occasions. Though they sip their port in close contiguity, they are poles asunder in their minds and feelings. When the Guestwick fly came for Mrs Eames, and the parson's pony-phaeton came for him and Mrs Boyce, a great relief was felt; but the misery of those who were left had gone too far to allow of any reaction on that evening. The squire yawned, and the earl yawned, and then there was an end of it for that night.

Anthony Trollope, *The Small House at Allington*, 1864

The Greys had just come from Windsor Castle. Lady Grey, in her own *distressed* manner, said she was really more dead than alive. She said all the boring she had ever endured before was literally nothing compared with her misery of the two preceding nights. She hoped she never should see a mahogany table again, she was so tired with the one that the Queen and the King, the Duchess of Gloucester, Princess Augusta, Madame Lieven and herself had sat round for *hours* – the Queen knitting or netting a purse – the King sleeping, and occasionally waking for the purpose of saying: – 'Exactly so, ma'am!' and then sleeping again. The Queen was cold as ice to Lady Grey, till the moment she came away, when she could afford to be a little civil at getting quit of her. . . .

We asked Lord Grey how he had passed his evening: 'I played at whist,' said he, 'and what is more, I won £2, which I never did before.' . . . At dinner Lady Grey sat between Talleyrand and Esterhazy. I, at some little distance, commanded a full view of her face, and was sure of her *thoughts*; for, as you know, she hates Talleyrand, and he was making the cursedest nasty noises in his throat.

Thomas Creevey, letter to Miss Ord, 1833

The king that Thomas Creevey refers to is William IV. His habits were a far cry from those of the Prince Regent, afterwards George IV, his immediate predecessor. Thomas Creevey's wife decided that only the political advantage of being the Prince and Mrs Fitzherbert's guest could possibly justify the strain of Pavilion life.

Brighton, Oct. 29th, 1805

Oh, this wicked Pavilion! we were there till ½ past one this morng., and it has kept me in bed with the headache till 12 to-day. . . . The invitation did not come to us till 9 o'clock: we went in Lord Thurlow's carriage, and were in fear of being too late; but the Prince did not come out of the dining-room till 11. Till then our only companions were Lady Downshire and Mr and Miss Johnstone – the former very goodnatured and amiable. . . . When the Prince appeared, I instantly saw he had got more wine than usual, and it was still more evident that the German Baron was extremely drunk. The Prince came up and sat by me – introduced McMahon to me, and talked a great deal about Mrs Fitzherbert – said she had been 'delighted' with my note, and wished much to see me. He asked her 'When?' – and he said her answer was – 'Not till *you* are gone, and I can see her *comfortably*.' . . .

Afterwards the Prince led all the party to the table where the maps lie, to see him shoot with an air-gun at a target placed at the end of the room. He did it very skilfully, and wanted all the ladies to attempt it. The girls and I excused ourselves on account of our short sight; but Lady Downshire hit a fiddler in the dining-room, Miss Johnstone a door and Bloomfield the ceiling. . . . I soon had enough of this, and retired to the fire with Mac. . . . At last a waltz was played by the band, and the Prince offered to waltz with Miss Johnstone, but very quietly, and once round the table made him giddy, so of course it was proper for his partner to be giddy too; but he cruelly only thought of supporting himself, so she reclined on the Baron.

Mrs Creevey, letter to Thomas Creevey, 1805

Since conventional hospitality quickly loses its interest for people who entertain too often, aristocratic and fashionable hosts are often found resorting to more perverse amusements, or the extremes of casualness. 'Freak dinners' became a fad on both sides of the Atlantic during the Edwardian era.

The New York smart set is still talking of nothing but Mrs Bernheimer's topsy-turvy dinner which began with coffee and ended with soups and oysters, the guests sitting on the table. It is considered the wittiest idea that a member of the New York Smart Set has had for years.

Punch

The sort of hospitality offered by Lord Melbourne is, of course, common among unconventional, or inefficient, hosts of all classes and periods.

I hear they wander about there [Lord Melbourne's] all day and sleep about all the evening; no meal is at a given hour, but drops upon them as an unexpected pleasure.

Harriet, Countess of Granville, letter to Lady Morpeth, 1811

*Even conventional amusements can make a visit a night-
mare to a guest who simply does not want them. The poet
Thomas Gray's friendship with Miss Speed never
recovered from this visit.*

She asked him to stay with her, but then changed the
date of his visit several times to suit her whim, a most
disturbing thing to a man who liked to know his exact
plans months beforehand. And then when he did
arrive, she plunged him into a vortex of social activity.
'I am come to my resting-place,' he wrote tartly once
he was safe back at Cambridge, 'and find it very
necessary after living for a month in a house with
three women, that laughed from morning to night and
would allow nothing to the sulkiness of my disposition.
Company and cards at home, parties by land and water;
and what they call *doing something*, that is racketting
about from morning to night, are occupations, I find,
that wear out my spirits.'

David Cecil, Two Quiet Lives, 1948

Charles Ryder's father, in Evelyn Waugh's Brideshead
Revisited, *employs a perversity which amounts to a kind
of black hostmanship, in a subtle battle to get his son to
leave home. Charles Ryder has spent his allowance during
the previous university term, and is now forced by lack of
funds to spend the vacation sparring with his father.*

Next day, by chance, a weapon came to hand. I met an
old acquaintance of school-days, a contemporary of
mine named Jorkins. I never had much liking for
Jorkins. . . . Now I greeted him with enthusiasm and
asked him to dinner. He came and showed little
alteration. My father must have been warned by Hayter
that there was a guest, for instead of his velvet suit he
wore a tail coat; this, with a black waistcoat, very high
collar, and very narrow white tie, was his evening

dress. . . . He never possessed a dinner jacket.

'Good evening, good evening. So nice of you to come all this way.'

'Oh, it wasn't far,' said Jorkins, who lived in Sussex Square.

'Science annihilates distance,' said my father disconcertingly. 'You are over here on business?'

'Well, I'm *in* business, if that's what you mean.'

'I had a cousin who was in business – you wouldn't know him; it was before your time. I was telling Charles about him only the other night. He has been much in my mind. He came', my father paused to give full weight to the bizarre word – 'a *cropper*.'

Jorkins giggled nervously. My father fixed him with a look of reproach.

'You find his misfortune the subject of mirth? Or perhaps the word I used was unfamiliar; *you* no doubt would say that he "folded up".'

My father was master of the situation. He had made a little fantasy for himself, that Jorkins should be an American, and throughout the evening he played a delicate, one-sided parlour-game with him, explaining any peculiarly English terms that occurred in the conversation, translating pounds into dollars, and courteously deferring to him with such phrases as 'Of course, by *your* standards . . .'; 'All this must seem very parochial to Mr Jorkins'; 'In the vast spaces to which *you* are accustomed . . .' so that my guest was left with the vague sense that there was a misconception somewhere as to his identity, which he never got the chance of explaining. Again and again during dinner he sought my father's eye, thinking to read there the simple statement that this form of address was an elaborate joke, but met instead a look of such mild benignity that he was left baffled. . . .

At the door of the dining-room he left us. 'Good

night, Mr Jorkins,' he said. 'I hope you will pay us another visit when you next "cross the herring pond".'

'I say, what did your governor mean by that? He seemed almost to think I was American.'

'He's rather odd at times.'

'I mean all that about advising me to visit Westminster Abbey. It seemed rum.'

'Yes. I can't quite explain.'

'I almost thought he was pulling my leg,' said Jorkins in puzzled tones.

My father's counter-attack was delivered a few days later. He sought me out and said, 'Mr Jorkins is still here?'

'No, father, of course not. He only came to dinner.'

'Oh, I hoped he was staying with us. Such a *versatile* young man.'

Evelyn Waugh, Brideshead Revisited, 1945

THE SNUG LITTLE BED

Freddie Widgeon is a typical Wodehouse young man: charming, upper-class, slow-witted, and a bachelor. Dahlia Prenderby has invited him to her parents' home for the weekend, but his conversation on the first evening gets off to a bad start.

'Charming place you have here, what?'

Lady Prenderby said that the local scenery was generally admired. She was one of those tall, rangy, Queen Elizabeth sort of women, with tight lips and cold, blanc-mange-y eyes. Freddie didn't like her looks much, but he was feeling fairly fizzy, so he carried on with a bright zip.

'Pretty good hunting country, I should think?'

'I believe there is a good deal of hunting near here, yes.'

'I thought as much,' said Freddie. 'Ah, that's the stuff, is it not? A cracking gallop across good country with a jolly fine kill at the end of it, what, what? Hark for'ard, yoicks, tally-ho, I mean to say, and all that sort of thing.'

Lady Prenderby shivered austerely.

'I fear I cannot share your enthusiasm,' she said. 'I have the strongest possible objection to hunting. I have always set my face against it, as against all similar brutalizing blood-sports.'

This was a nasty jar for poor old Freddie, who had been relying on the topic to carry him nicely through at least a couple of courses. It silenced him for the nonce. And as he paused to collect his faculties, his host, who had now been glowering for six and a half minutes practically without cessation, put a hand in front of his mouth and addressed the girl Dahlia across the table. Freddie thinks he was under the impression that he was speaking in a guarded whisper, but, as a matter of fact, the words boomed through the air as if he had been a costermonger calling attention to his Brussels sprouts.

'Dahlia!'

'Yes, Father?'

'Who's that ugly feller?'

'Hush!'

'What do you mean, hush? Who is he?'

'Mr Widgeon.'

'Mr Who?'

'Widgeon.'

'I wish you would articulate clearly and not mumble,' said Sir Mortimer fretfully. 'It sounds to me just like

[54]

"Widgeon". Who asked him here?'

'I did.'

'Why?'

'He's a friend of mine.'

'Well, he looks a pretty frightful young slab of damnation to me. What I'd call a criminal face.'

'Hush!'

'Why do you keep saying "Hush"? . . . How long's he staying?'

'Till Monday.'

'My God! And to-day's only Friday!' bellowed Sir Mortimer Prenderby.

P. G. Wodehouse, Young Men in Spats, 1936

Weekending with a girl's parents could be just as daunting in real life. Lord Redesdale, 'Farve', father of the Mitford sisters, terrorizes his guests as much in Jessica Mitford's autobiography as in Nancy Mitford's fiction, such as Highland Fling.

'You *can't* publish that under your own name,' my mother insisted, scandalized, for not only did thinly disguised aunts, uncles and family friends people the pages of *Highland Fling*, but there, larger than life-size, felicitously named 'General Murgatroyd', was Farve. . . . The General was portrayed as an ardent organizer of shooting parties, a man of violent temper, terror of housemaids and gamekeepers, who spent most of his time inveighing against the Huns and growling at various languid, aesthetic young men in pastel silk shirts who kept popping up at unexpected moments. My father's peculiar argot – 'Damn sewer!' 'Stinks to merry hell!' – his loathing of anything or anyone who smacked of the literary or the artistic, were drawn to the life. . . .

The languid young aesthetes of *Highland Fling* also turned up frequently in real life, imported by Nancy, as visitors at Swinbrook. Most of these had the effect on Farve of driving him into a Murgatroydish rage; to one or two, he took an unaccountable liking. Which was the worse fate – to be loathed or liked – was somewhat of a toss-up, since to remain in good odour required such substantial sacrifices as taking part in week-end shooting parties and being down for breakfast promptly at eight o'clock.

'Brains for breakfast, Mark!' Farve roared genially at one of his capriciously chosen favourites, who, to maintain status, had staggered uncertainly into the dining-room, looking haggard and drooping, on the dot of eight. The standard aesthete's breakfast was a *cachet Faivre*, nearest thing to a tranquillizer in those days, and a glass of orange juice or China tea, taken at about noon.

Poor Mark turned a delicate shade of chartreuse, excused himself, and was heard violently retching in the nearest w.c. This incident, too, passed in its turn into part of the mythology of Farve. To celebrate it Debo and I promptly made up a Honnish song, a sort of signature tune for Mark, to be sung whenever he came to Swinbrook, with the lugubrious chorus: 'Brains for Breakfast, Mark! Brains for Breakfast, Mark! Oh, the damn sewer! Oh, the damn sewer!'

Jessica Mitford, *Hons and Rebels*, 1960

Aesthetes, young men from Oxford, were a regular ingredient in Lady Ottoline Morrell's house-parties at Garsington. Anthony Powell first visited Garsington as an undergraduate, at a time when one of the regular guests was Maurice Bowra, then a young don and something of a social virtuoso.

Garsington conditions have often been described, emphasis usually laid on the exotic appearance and behaviour of the hostess, both of which certainly had to be reckoned with. The worst perplexities always seemed to me to lie rather in the utter uncertainty as to what level of life there was to be assumed by the guest....

At Garsington one more or less wild man was likely to be present, a bohemian exhibit (in Wyndham Lewis's phrase, an Ape of God), making appropriately bohemian remarks. To have these comments addressed to oneself, especially during the many silences that fell, was something to be dreaded. Alternatively, you might be caught out, in quite a different manner, by forgetting, say, the date of Ascot, or the name of some nobleman's 'place'. On the whole the legend of imposing intellectual conversation was the least of Garsington's threats....

Even Bowra was prepared to recognize that an invitation to Garsington was not a matter to be treated lightly. For the most experienced in salon life, it represented moving up to the front line; for a nervous undergraduate, an ordeal of the most gruelling order. Bowra, staying once in the house, coming down to breakfast early, had inadvertently eaten the toast (possibly Ryvita, even if toast, toast of some special sort) found in the toast-rack. A short time later Lady Ottoline arrived. She looked round the table. Something was wrong. She rang the bell.

'Where is my toast?'

Lady Ottoline's very individual way of speaking, a kind of ominous cooing nasal hiss – often imitated, but, like Goodhart's whinny, never altogether successfully – was at its most threatening. The parlourmaid (also a formidable figure, addressed by name, which I do not remember) fixed her eyes on Bowra.

'The toast was there when *he* came down, m'lady ...'

To Keep the Ball Rolling, the Memoirs of Anthony Powell,
Volume I, *Infants of the Spring*, 1976

*There are also hosts who strike terror into their guests
with silence. Several accounts exist of the kindly-meant
but nevertheless fearsome hospitality offered by Benjamin
Jowett, 'The Jowler', while he was Master of Balliol
College, Oxford, from 1870 to 1893.*

During the whole four years I was up I scarcely passed
a term without being invited to a solitary meal with
him, either breakfast or dinner. The time passed in
almost complete silence. Now and again I used to
venture an embarrassed remark, but as likely as not the
reply would be, 'You wouldn't have said that if you'd
stopped to think', and after a silence more glacial
still he dismissed me with a brief 'Good morning'.

J. A. Spender, in *Oxford*, 1936

*As another instance of the sort of remark from which a
guest can scarcely recover, here is a story told by Edward
Lear of the time when he gave drawing lessons to Queen
Victoria.*

The Queen was showing him the priceless Royal
collection of miniatures. Lear was so completely
absorbed in studying them that, in the excitement of
the moment, he quite forgot where he was and exclaimed, 'Oh! where *did* you get all these beautiful
things?' – as though Her Majesty had 'picked them
up' at an antique shop. The Queen's answer, as he
remarked, was an excellent one, kind, but dignified
and completely conclusive: 'I inherited them, Mr
Lear.'

Angus Davidson, *Edward Lear*, 1938

We come now to apologetic, inadequate, and worried hosts.

I'm afraid it's only a scratch meal, but –

– we'll have sandwiches after the meeting
– I'm between maids

– something went wrong with the stew
– Caroline's been a real little devil
– I wasn't sure you'd remember to come
– the butcher didn't send
– it was that or my Girl Guides
– personally I can never manage anything before a
    lecture
– when you think that before the war
– there's plenty of macaroni – I've only to open a tin
– I forgot it was half-day closing
– we usually have our big meal at lunchtime
– I do hope you can eat eel
– it's all the less to wash up
– what I say is, it's not the food that counts but the
    company
– we'd got so many bits to finish up
– home's always nicer than a restaurant
– we *are* eating in the dining-room
– the tulips are our own
– we're having my own version of something we found
    in a little peasant hut in Bukovina
– it won't be long now
– I knew you wouldn't mind.

Marghanita Laski, Apologies, 1955

Druitt ceased to be interested in appearing clever. So
he decided to be wealthy instead. He gave innumerable
meals. They were not very good, but they were free.
Druitt had no manner as a host. He couldn't put people
at their ease, but he was solicitous and conscientious.
He went round filling up glasses before they were half
empty. His preoccupation with the distribution of food
prevented his joining in conversations intelligently.
There were often pauses, which Druitt tried to bridge
over by looking benevolent and worried. He always
seemed to be just not equal to the occasion, struggling,
you know. He relied immensely on the co-operation of

his guests. He used to remind me of a waiter from a second-rate establishment, very eager and willing, but clumsy.

L. P. Hartley, *A Beautiful Character*, 1924

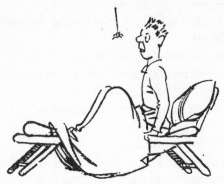

THE SOCIABLE SPIDER

'O, Ratty!' he cried dismally, 'why ever did I do it? Why did I bring you to this poor, cold little place, on a night like this, when you might have been at River Bank by this time, toasting your toes before a blazing fire, with all your own nice things about you!'

The Rat paid no heed to his doleful self-reproaches. He was running here and there, opening doors, inspecting rooms and cupboards, and lighting lamps and candles and sticking them up everywhere. 'What a capital little house this is!' he called out cheerily. 'So compact! So well planned! Everything here and everything in its place! We'll make a jolly night of it. The first thing we want is a good fire; I'll see to that – I always know where to find things. So this is the parlour? Splendid! Your own idea, those little sleeping-bunks in the wall? Capital! Now, I'll fetch the wood and the coals, and you get a duster, Mole – you'll find one in the drawer of the kitchen table – and try and smarten things up a bit. Bustle about, old chap!'

Encouraged by his inspiriting companion, the Mole

roused himself and dusted and polished with energy and heartiness, while the Rat, running to and fro with armfuls of fuel, soon had a cheerful blaze roaring up the chimney. He hailed the Mole to come and warm himself; but Mole promptly had another fit of the blues, dropping down on a couch in dark despair and burying his face in his duster.

'Rat,' he moaned, 'how about your supper, you poor, cold, hungry, weary animal? I've nothing to give you – nothing – not a crumb!'

'What a fellow you are for giving in!' said the Rat reproachfully. 'Why, only just now I saw a sardine-opener on the kitchen dresser, quite distinctly; and everybody knows that means there are sardines about somewhere in the neighbourhood. Rouse yourself! pull yourself together, and come with me and forage.'

They went and foraged accordingly, hunting through every cupboard and turning out every drawer. The result was not so very depressing after all, though of course it might have been better; a tin of sardines – a box of captain's biscuits, nearly full – and a German sausage encased in silver paper.

'There's a banquet for you!' observed the Rat, as he arranged the table. 'I know some animals who would give their ears to be sitting down to supper with us to-night!'

'No bread!' groaned the Mole dolorously; 'no butter, no—'

'No *pâté de foie gras*, no champagne!' continued the Rat, grinning. 'And that reminds me – what's that little door at the end of the passage? Your cellar, of course! Every luxury in this house! Just you wait a minute.'

He made for the cellar door, and presently re-appeared, somewhat dusty, with a bottle of beer in each paw and another under each arm. 'Self-indulgent beggar you seem to be, Mole,' he observed. 'Deny yourself nothing. This is really the jolliest little place I ever was in.'

Kenneth Grahame, *The Wind in the Willows*, 1908

In spite of owing much rent to his landlady Mrs Raddle, Bob Sawyer in Pickwick Papers *gives an evening party at his lodgings, with Mr Allen, Mr Hopkins and Mr Pickwick among the guests.*

Mr Bob Sawyer rang for supper, and the visitors squeezed themselves into corners while it was getting ready. . . . The man to whom the order for the oysters had been sent, had not been told to open them; it is a very difficult thing to open an oyster with a limp knife or a two-pronged fork; and very little was done in this way. Very little of the beef was done either; and the ham (which was also from the German-sausage shop round the corner) was in a similar predicament. However, there was plenty of porter in a tin can; and the cheese went a great way, for it was very strong. So upon the whole, perhaps, the supper was quite as good as such matters usually are.

After supper, another jug of punch was put upon the table, together with a paper of cigars, and a couple of bottles of spirits. Then, there was an awful pause; and this awful pause was occasioned by a very common occurrence in this sort of place, but a very embarrassing one notwithstanding. . . .

The sight of the tumblers restored Bob Sawyer to a degree of equanimity which he had not possessed since his interview with his landlady. His face brightened up, and he began to feel quite convivial.

'Now, Betsy,' said Mr Bob Sawyer, with great suavity, and dispersing, at the same time, the tumultuous little mob of glasses the girl had collected in the centre of the table: 'now, Betsy, the warm water; be brisk, there's a good girl.'

'You can't have no warm water,' replied Betsy.

'No warm water!' exclaimed Mr Bob Sawyer.

'No,' said the girl, with a shake of the head which expressed a more decided negative than the most copious language could have conveyed. 'Missis Raddle said you warn't to have none.'

The surprise depicted on the countenances of his guests imparted new courage to the host.

'Bring up the warm water instantly – instantly!' said Mr Bob Sawyer, with desperate sternness.

'No. I can't,' replied the girl; 'Missis Raddle raked out the kitchen fire afore she went to bed, and locked up the kittle.'

'Oh, never mind; never mind. Pray don't disturb yourself about such a trifle,' said Mr Pickwick, observing the conflict of Bob Sawyer's passions, as depicted in his countenance, 'cold water will do very well.'

'Oh, admirably,' said Mr Benjamin Allen.

'My landlady is subject to some slight attacks of mental derangement,' remarked Bob Sawyer with a ghastly smile; 'And I fear I must give her warning.'

'No, don't,' said Ben Allen.

'I fear I must,' said Bob with heroic firmness. 'I'll pay her what I owe her, and give her warning to-morrow morning.' Poor fellow! how devoutly he wished he could!...

'Now,' said Jack Hopkins, 'just to set us going again, Bob, I don't mind singing a song.' And Hopkins, incited thereto, by tumultuous applause, plunged himself at once into 'The King, God bless him,' which he sang as loud as he could, to a novel air, compounded of the 'Bay of Biscay', and 'A Frog he would'. The chorus was the essence of the song; and, as each gentleman sang it to the tune he knew best, the effect was very striking indeed.

It was at the end of the chorus to the first verse, that Mr Pickwick held up his hand in a listening attitude, and said, as soon as silence was restored:

'Hush! I beg your pardon. I thought I heard somebody calling from up stairs.'

A profound silence immediately ensued; and Mr Bob Sawyer was observed to turn pale.

'I think I hear it now,' said Mr Pickwick. 'Have the goodness to open the door.'

The door was no sooner opened than all doubt on the subject was removed.

'Mr Sawyer! Mr Sawyer!' screamed a voice from the two-pair landing.

'It's my landlady,' said Bob Sawyer, looking round him with great dismay. 'Yes, Mrs Raddle.'

'What do you mean by this, Mr Sawyer?' replied the voice, with great shrillness and rapidity of utterance. 'Ain't it enough to be swindled out of one's rent, and money lent out of pocket besides, and abused and insulted by your friends that dares to call themselves men: without having the house turned out of window, and noise enough made to bring the fire-engines here, at two o'clock in the morning? – Turn them wretches away.'...

'They're going, Mrs Raddle, they're going,' said the miserable Bob. 'I am afraid you'd better go,' said Mr Bob Sawyer to his friends. 'I *thought* you were making too much noise.'

Charles Dickens, *Pickwick Papers*, 1836–7

There is an odd incident in Johnson's Life of Swift. *The poet Pope and John Gay the composer were close friends of Dean Swift; and his behaviour on one occasion, when they called on him unexpectedly, struck Pope as memorably eccentric, even for that strange satirist.*

One evening, Gay and I went to see him: you know

how intimately we were all acquainted. On our coming
in, 'Heyday, gentlemen (says the Doctor), what's the
meaning of this visit? How come you to leave all the
great Lords, that you are so fond of, to come hither to
see a poor Dean?' – 'Because we would rather see you
than any of them.' – 'Aye, any one that did not know
you so well as I do, might believe you. But since you
are come, I must get some supper for you, I suppose.' –
'No, Doctor, we have supped already.' – 'Supped
already? that's impossible! why, 'tis not eight o'clock
yet. – That's very strange; but, if you had not supped,
I must have got something for you. – Let me see, what
should I have had? A couple of lobsters: aye, that would
have done very well; two shillings – tarts, a shilling:
but you will drink a glass of wine with me, though you
supped so much before your usual time only to spare
my pocket?' – 'No, we had rather talk with you than
drink with you.' – 'But if you had supped with me, as
in all reason you ought to have done, you must have
drunk with me. – A bottle of wine, two shillings – two
and two is four, and one is five: just two-and-sixpence
a-piece. There, Pope, there's half a crown for you,
and there's another for you, Sir; for I won't save any
thing by you, I am determined.' – This was all said
and done with his usual seriousness on such occasions;
and, in spite of every thing we could say to the contrary, he actually obliged us to take the money.

Alexander Pope, quoted in Samuel Johnson,
Lives of the Poets, 1779–81

*Hosts who fail to give their guests enough to eat or drink
divide into the frugal and the mean; but whereas the mean
host breaks the most ancient codes of hospitality, and is
a clear target for ridicule, the frugal entertainer inspires
confused admiration. Certainly he can be faulted for the
unconvivial atmosphere that hangs around him, but the*

*reason is that his mind is on higher things. The guest
therefore feels inferior, a guilty hedonist.*

*The biographer Michael Holroyd's visit to Lytton
Strachey's brother James was already thoroughly disconcerting, even before the meal began. Both James
Strachey and his wife were psychoanalysts, and James
looked almost exactly like Freud. He also left such silences
that Holroyd found himself 'jabbering nonsense' to fill the
spaces in the conversation before lunch.*

His wife came in, austere and intellectual, very thin,
with a deeply-lined parchment face and large deeply
expressive eyes. We all drank a little pale sherry and
then moved in procession past a sculptured bust of
Lytton to the dining-room.

Lunch was a spartan affair. Though extremely
generous in spirit, my hosts were by temperament
ascetic, and lived very frugally. We ate spam, a cold
potato each, and lettuce leaves. In our glasses there
showed a faint blush of red wine from the Wine
Society, but I was the only one who so much as sipped
any. My hosts solemnly tipped theirs down the sink
at the conclusion of the meal. After the spam, some
cheese was quarried out from the cold storage, and
some biscuits extracted from a long row of numbered
tins ranged like files along a shelf in the kitchen.
Everything, spam, potato, lettuce, cheese and biscuits,
was, like the windows, swathed in protective cello-
phane.

During lunch we talked of psychoanalysis – not the
subject but the word, its derivation and correct
spelling. Should it have a hyphen? Did it need both
the central 'o' and 'a'? It was a topic to which I could
contribute little of brilliance.

After lunch, Alix Strachey excused herself. She was
going upstairs to watch a television programme for

children. Recently she had decided to learn physics, she explained for my benefit, and found these kindergarten classes very instructive. James said nothing. In silence we filed back the biscuits on the shelf, poured away the rest of the wine, re-inserted the cheese into its wrappings and into its frozen chamber. Then James announced that we were to visit the 'studio wilderness', a large building with a stone floor, standing some ten yards to the rear of the house. He put on boots, a scarf, gloves, a heavy belted overcoat down to his ankles, and we started out on our journey.

Michael Holroyd, *Lytton Strachey : A Biography*, 1973

Anthony Powell's character Erridge, Lord Warminster, combines left-wing ideals with a vestige of ordinary upper-class stinginess; he continues to live in the family home, but ascetically. In this scene his sister Susan has arrived with friends and announced her engagement.

'I grant it may not be my place to say so,' Quiggin went on, switching at the same time to a somewhat rougher delivery. 'But you know, Alf, you really ought to celebrate rightly in a bottle of champagne. Now, don't you think there is some bubbly left in that cellar of yours?' ...

Erridge was undoubtedly taken aback, although not, I think, on the ground that the suggestion came from Quiggin. Erridge did not traffic in individual psychology. It was an idea that was important to him, not its originator. The whole notion of drinking champagne because your sister was engaged was, in itself, obviously alien to him; alien both to his temperament and ideals. Champagne no doubt represented to his mind a world he had fled. ...

'I really cannot answer that question offhand,' Erridge said – and one caught a faint murmur of ancestral voices answering for the Government some awkward question raised by the Opposition – 'As you know I hardly ever drink anything myself, except an occasional glass of beer – certainly never champagne. To tell the truth, I hate the stuff. We'd better ask Smith.'

Smith, as it happened, appeared at that moment with coffee. Already he showed signs of being nervously disturbed by the arrival of the girls, his hands shaking visibly as he held the tray; so much so that some of the liquid spilled from the pot.

'Smith, is there any champagne left in the cellar?'

Erridge's voice admitted the exceptional nature of the enquiry. He asked almost apologetically. Even so, the shock was terrific. Smith started so violently that the coffee cups rattled on the tray. . . . After a long pause, he at last shook his head.

'I doubt if there is any champagne left, m'lord.'

'Oh, I'm sure there is, Smith, if you go and look,' said Susan. 'You see it is to celebrate my engagement, Smith. I'm going to get married.' . . .

He brought a bottle . . . It was Mumm, 1906: a magnum. Nothing could have borne out more thoroughly Erridge's statement about his own lack of interest in wine. It was, indeed, a mystery that this relic of former high living should have survived. . . .

'Just the one left,' said Smith.

He spoke in anguish, though not without resignation. Erridge hesitated. Almost as much as Smith, he seemed to dislike the idea of broaching the wine for the rest of us to drink. A moral struggle was raging within him.

'I don't know whether I really ought not to keep it,' he said. 'If there is only one. I mean, if someone or other turned up who —'

He found no individual worthy enough to name, because he stopped suddenly short.

'Oh, *do* let's, Alf,' said Mona. . . .

[68]

'Oh, yes,' said Erridge. 'You're right, Mona. We'll break its neck and celebrate your engagement, Sue.'

He was undoubtedly proud of fetching from somewhere deeply embedded in memory this convivial phrase; also cheered by the immediate, and quite general, agreement that now was the moment to drink so mature – so patriarchal – a vintage. Smith disappeared again. After another long delay he returned with champagne glasses, which had received a perfunctory rub to dispel dust accumulated since at least the time of Erridge's succession. Then, with the peculiar deftness of the alcoholic, he opened the bottle.

Anthony Powell, *At Lady Molly's*, 1957

'Elegant economy' is the motto of the village of Cranford, but in the character of the Honourable Mrs Jamieson economy shades into meanness, made worse by favouritism.

In a few minutes tea was brought. Very delicate was the china, very old the plate, very thin the bread and butter, and very small the lumps of sugar. Sugar was evidently Mrs Jamieson's favourite economy. I question if the little filigree sugar-tongs, made something like scissors, could have opened themselves wide enough to take up an honest, vulgar good-sized piece; and when I tried to seize two little minnikin pieces at once, so as not to be detected in too many returns to the sugar-basin, they absolutely dropped one, with a little sharp clatter, quite in a malicious and unnatural manner. But before this happened we had had a slight disappointment. In the little silver jug was cream, in the larger one was milk. As soon as Mr Mulliner came in, Carlo began to beg, which was a thing our manners forbade us to do, though I am sure we were just as hungry; and Mrs Jamieson said she was certain we would excuse her if she gave her poor dumb Carlo his tea first. She accordingly mixed a saucerful for him, and put it down for him to lap; and then she told us how intelligent and sensible the dear little fellow was; he knew cream quite well, and constantly refused tea with only milk in it: so the milk was left for us; but we silently thought we were quite as intelligent and sensible as Carlo, and felt as if insult were added to injury when we were called upon to admire the gratitude evinced by his wagging his tail for the cream which should have been ours.

Elizabeth Gaskell, *Cranford*, 1853

Ernest, in The One Before, *is obsessed by petty savings, but his tricks are from the standard repertoire of parsimonious hosts, mocked by Thackeray nearly a century earlier.*

'I've seen cook, Ernest, and she says the lamb won't do minced for luncheon. Not enough.'

'Strange,' said Ernest, caressing his chin. 'I was thinking as I carved it last night at dinner that it could be made to do very well.'

'Yes, Ernest; I saw you were.' She was guiltless of irony, and merely wished to agree with him. 'You see, when you get it off the bone —'

'Quite so. I'm sure I don't wish to stint anybody. I needn't say that. But all that is wanted is a little management. Tell cook to put the mince on toast, thick toast. And – well, some poached eggs on the top would make it look more of a dish perhaps. Eggs – I don't know what eggs are this week. They've been very dear lately. Never mind; pay, pay, pay! There's no end to it.'

'Are you quite sure, Ernest, that you like to have people staying at the house? Sometimes I think it seems to put you out a little. Of course it does add to expenditure.'

Without intending it, she had touched him on the raw. She had assailed his character as a host.

'Now, why you should say that, Mary, except to annoy me, I can't think. There is nothing I enjoy more than the exercise of hospitality within reasonable limits. I dislike recklessness; but what has that to do with it? I suppose you wish to imply that I am not a good host?'

'Of course that would be absurd, dear.'

'I should be extremely sorry for James, or any other guest of mine, to leave my house with the impression that he had not had enough to eat. The position of a host carries with it its duties. I feel that as a point of honour. It is like the old *noblesse oblige*. Now, with regard to the luncheon, let me think. Yes, we will have the pressed beef on the sideboard. There is no occasion for you to make any allusion to it; but have it there. If he wishes for it, he will mention it. James is like that. However, he is your brother-in-law's brother, and, after all, he leaves this afternoon; we must be rather more careful after he has gone.'

Barry Pain, *The One Before*, 1934

THE BATH IN THE BASIN

Poor Dinner-giving Snobs! you don't know what small thanks you get for all your pains and money! How we Dining-out Snobs sneer at your cookery, and pooh-pooh your old hock, and are incredulous about your four-and-sixpenny champagne; and know that the side-dishes of to-day are *réchauffés* from the dinner of yesterday, and mark how certain dishes are whisked off the table untasted, so that they may figure at the banquet to-morrow. Whenever, for my part, I see the head man particularly anxious to *escamoter* [whisk away] a fricandeau or a blancmange, I always call out, and insist upon massacring it with a spoon. All this sort of conduct makes one popular with the Dinner-giving Snob.

William Makepeace Thackeray, *A Book of Snobs*, 1847

Meanness is almost always tempered by hypocrisy, by the need to keep up appearances, so at least the guest gets something to eat. A high-principled host is considerably more dangerous, as appears in this story from Auden and Isherwood's travels in China.

Never forgetting our admiration for the missionaries of the Yellow River, it is only fair to tell the story we heard recently from an American airman in Hankow. Some years ago the airman and a friend were flying near Loyang. The weather shut down, so they made for the nearest emergency landing-field, on the outskirts of a small, dirty town. The airman suggested that they should try to get a bed at the mission-station, and, sure enough, the missionary received them hospitably, and showed them up to a bedroom, where they shaved, washed, and changed their clothes. They didn't see their host again until the evening. Downstairs, supper was ready: the food looked good, and they were both very hungry. Then the missionary, having said Grace, suddenly asked: 'Does either of you gentlemen smoke?'

The airman didn't, but his friend did. 'Do you drink?' Yes, they both took a drink occasionally. 'Then I'm sorry,' said the missionary, 'there's no place for you under this roof.' They could hardly believe their ears; but the missionary wasn't joking. Out they had to go, leaving the supper uneaten, to sleep on chairs in the local Chinese inn. 'And now tell me', our informant concluded, 'what would *you* have said to that missionary?'

W. H. Auden and Christopher Isherwood, *Journey to a War*, 1939

Here are further ways in which an intolerant host can torment a guest who smokes, or smokes at the wrong time.

One thing deters smoking, we discovered, and that is to keep some very stale filter-tip Gauloises to offer people when they have run out of, or forgotten to bring, their own cigarettes.

We tell them the Gauloises are straight off the Dieppe-Newhaven boat. So they were – eight years ago. In desperation they accept your offer. Nobody ever smokes more than one, and lives to tell the tale.

Spike Hughes, *The Art of Coarse Entertaining*, 1972

There was once-upon-a-time – or, because we have heard the story ascribed to three different Dukes, perhaps thrice-upon-a-time – a Duke who did not tolerate smoking during dinner, though he had many American acquaintances. Once, and once only, one of these lit a cigarette as soon as the soup-plates were removed. The Duke called his butler. 'You will now serve coffee' he commanded, and that was the end of the meal.

Francis Meynell, *The Weekend Book*, 1955

Finally, here are two instances of sheer malice in a host, the first of the most gentle, the second of the most lethal kind.

Margaret Craven's novel concerns a North American Indian community on the Canadian coast receiving a new vicar, a white man.

In one of the best houses of the village Mrs Hudson, the matriarch, was pleased that a vicar was again in residence. The Bishop would surely come more frequently, perhaps even with a boatload of landlubber clergy to be fed and housed, and the young wives would gather here in her house to defer to her judgement, speaking softly in Kwákwala.

'What meat shall we have?'

'Roast beef. Or salmon. Or wild goose. Or duck.'

'And what vegetable shall we have?' Mrs Hudson's answer was always the same, and her small revenge on the white man, the intruder.

'Mashed turnips.' No white man liked mashed turnips.

Margaret Craven, I Heard the Owl Call My Name, 1967

The Borgias selected and laid down rare poisons in their cellars with as much thought as they gave to their vintage wines. Extraordinary! – but the Romans do not seem to have thought so. An invitation to dine at the Palazzo Borghese was accounted the highest social honour. I am aware that in recent books of Italian history there has been a tendency to whiten the Borgias' characters. But I myself hold to the old romantic black way of looking at the Borgias. I maintain that though you would often in the fifteenth century have heard the snobbish Roman say, in a would-be off-hand tone, 'I am dining with the Borgias to-night', no Roman ever was able to say 'I dined last night with the Borgias'.

Max Beerbohm, Hosts and Guests, 1920

Time to Leave

It was a delightful visit – perfect in being much too short.

Jane Austen, Emma, 1816

My father used to say,
'Superior people never make long visits,
have to be shown Longfellow's grave
or the glass flowers at Harvard.
Self-reliant like the cat –
that takes its prey to privacy,
the mouse's limp tail hanging like a shoelace from its
     mouth –
they sometimes enjoy solitude,
and can be robbed of speech
by speech which has delighted them.
The deepest feeling always shows itself in silence;
not in silence, but restraint.'
Nor was he insincere in saying, 'Make my house your
     inn.'
Inns are not residences.

Marianne Moore, from Observations, 1924

Etiquette books abound with advice on knowing when to leave, and anecdotes abound of guests who stay too long. The problem is age-old and intractable.

In its heyday, the short call was rigidly controlled, and the full weight of society protected hosts from 'visitations'. But as early as 1851 Mrs Gaskell had doubts about the value of the rules.

We now come to calls of *courtesy* or general calls. These

[75]

are paid between the hours of 3 and 6 p.m., to allow the luncheon to be well over and preparation for dinner to be easily arranged. . . . Visitors should never prolong their call beyond a quarter of an hour or twenty minutes if they wish to avoid the charge of having inflicted 'a visitation'.

Everybody's Everyday Reference Book, 1905

Then there were rules and regulations for visiting and calls; and they were announced to any young people who might be staying in the town, with all the solemnity with which the old Manx laws were read once a year on the Tinwald Mount.

'Our friends have sent to inquire how you are after your journey to-night, my dear' (fifteen miles in a gentleman's carriage); 'they will give you some rest to-morrow, but the next day, I have no doubt, they will call; so be at liberty after twelve – from twelve to three are our calling hours.'

Then, after they had called:

'It is the third day; I dare say your mamma has told you, my dear, never to let more than three days elapse between receiving a call and returning it; and also, that you are never to stay longer than a quarter of an hour.'

'But am I to look at my watch? How am I to find out when a quarter of an hour has passed?'

'You must keep thinking about the time, my dear, and not allow yourself to forget it in conversation.'

As everybody had this rule in their minds, whether they received or paid a call, of course no absorbing subject was ever spoken about. We kept ourselves to short sentences of small talk, and were punctual to our time.

Elizabeth Gaskell, *Cranford*, 1853

There is astonishing agreement throughout widely different periods and cultures on three days being the most a guest can be tolerated. (The exact interpretation of 'three days' varies: in some cultures it could mean just the days of arrival and departure and the intervening night.) These are merely a few of the appearances of the three-day rule.

No guest is so welcome in a friend's house that he will not become a nuisance after three days.

Plautus (*c.* 254–184 BC), *Miles Gloriosus*

Fish and visitors smell in three days.

Benjamin Franklin, *Poor Richard's Almanack*, 1735

The first day a man is a guest, the second a burden, the third a pest.

Edouard Laboulaye, *Abdallah*, 1859

After three days give a guest a rake.

Swahili proverb

Once such a convenient rule-of-thumb has been abandoned, the visitor has the far more embarrassing task of making his own enquiries, or understanding hints.

Two short visits tell better than one long one, looking as though you have been approved of. You can easily find out from the butler or the groom of the chambers, or some of the upper servants, how long you are expected to stay.

Ask Mama, 1858

There is always a risk of outstaying your welcome. Sad indeed would it be if it happened to you as to the visitor of whom the old Scotch lady said to the cook in his hearing: 'Jane, bile an extra egg for Mr Brown's breakfast the morn, for he is gaun to traivel.'

Everybody's Everyday Reference Book, 1905

Lancelot Phelps, Provost of Oriel College, Oxford, devised this donnish way of bringing his tea-parties to a close. His guests were undergraduates, who are notorious for being too shy to announce they are leaving ; I know of one don's wife who was left to wind up an undergraduate tea-party while her husband went to chapel ; she grew so desperate for conversation as the evening wore on that she was reduced to tearing up and burning old underwear in the grate, so as to comment on the different colours of the flames. Phelps's device seems scarcely less desperate.

He would lead the conversation towards some athletic topic, from this to the college games field, and from this again to the subject of badgers – which he would aver, quite baselessly, to have established a set endangering the cricket pitch. He would then recall Sir Thomas Browne's holding in debate whether or not badgers have longer legs on one side than the other, this the more readily to scamper round hills. Next, he would suddenly recall that a portrait of a badger hung somewhere in the Lodging, from which the truth of this matter might conceivably be verified. The picture would be located after a walk through the ramifying house; the badger would be seen to be equipped as other quadrupeds are; and then one would discover that the picture hung beside the Provost's front door, which stood open before one.

J. I. M. Stewart, in *My Oxford*, 1977

The following method seems quicker, but more chancy.

Empty all the ashtrays in a pointed manner; stay standing.

One host I heard of appears to fall asleep; he then wakes with a jerk and says, 'Darling, I think we should be going now.' Alas, I suppose you couldn't work it too often.

Katharine Whitehorn, *Whitehorn's Social Survival*, 1968

THE SUDDENLY-REMEMBERED APPOINTMENT

Mr Soapy Sponge's acceptance of an entirely unmeant invitation to stay with the Jawleyfords appears on page 4. Before long, Jawleyford is thinking of every possible way of getting rid of Sponge; not, as it turns out, at all an easy task. The chapter is entitled 'Bolting the Badger'.

'I wish he was off,' observed Jawleyford, after a pause. 'He bothers me excessively – I'll try and get rid of him by saying we are going from home.'

'Where can you say we are going to?' asked Mrs Jawleyford.

'Oh, anywhere,' replied Jawleyford; 'he doesn't know the people about here: the Tewkesburys', the Woolertons', the Browns', – anybody.'

Before they had got any definite plan of proceeding arranged, Mr Sponge returned from the chase.

'Ah, my dear sir!' exclaimed Jawleyford, half gaily, half moodily, extending a couple of fingers as Sponge entered his study: 'We thought you had taken French leave of us, and were off. . . . Why, my Lord Barker, a great friend of ours – known him from a boy – just like brothers, in short – sent over this morning to ask us all there – shooting party, charades, that sort of thing – and we accepted.'

[79]

'But that need make no difference,' replied Sponge; 'I'll go too.'

Jawleyford was taken aback. He had not calculated upon so much coolness.

'Well,' stammered he, 'that might do, to be sure; but – if – I'm not quite sure that I could take any one –'

'But if you're as thick as you say, you can have no difficulty,' replied our friend.

'True,' replied Jawleyford; 'but then we go a large party ourselves – two and two's four,' said he, 'to say nothing of servants; besides, his lordship mayn't have room – house will most likely be full.'

'Oh, a single man can always be put up; shakedown – anything does for him,' replied Sponge . . .

'Well,' replied Jawleyford . . . 'I'll talk to Mrs Jawleyford, and see if we can get off the Barkington expedition.'

'But don't get off on my account,' replied Sponge. 'I can stay here quite well. I dare say you'll not be away long.'

This was worse still; it held out no hope of getting rid of him. Jawleyford therefore resolved to try and smoke and starve him out. When our friend went to dress, he found his old apartment, the state-room, put away, the heavy brocade curtains brown-hollanded, the jugs turned upside down, the bed stripped of its clothes and the looking-glass laid a-top of it.

The smirking housemaid, who was just rolling the fire-irons up in the hearth-rug, greeted him with a 'Please, sir, we've shifted you into the brown room, east' . . .

A great change had come over everything. The fare, the lights, the footmen, the everything, underwent grievous diminution. The lamps were extinguished, and the transparent wax gave way to Palmer's com-

posites. . . . Mr Sponge, on his part, saw that all things
portended a close.

R. S. Surtees, *Mr Sponge's Sporting Tour*, 1853

*At William Randolph Hearst's ranch in California, the
hint that it was time to leave was dropped as part of the
routine. P. G. Wodehouse experienced the whole relentless
system on a visit in 1931.*

The house is enormous, and there are always at least
fifty guests staying there. All the furniture is period,
and you probably sleep on a bed originally occupied
by Napoleon or somebody. Ethel and I shared the
Venetian suite with Sidney Blackmer, who had blown
in from one of the studios.

The train that takes guests away leaves after mid-
night, and the one that brings new guests arrives early
in the morning, so you have dinner with one lot of
people and come down to breakfast next morning to
find an entirely fresh crowd.

Meals are in an enormous room, and are served at a
long table, with Hearst sitting in the middle on one side
and Marion Davies in the middle on the other. The
longer you are there, the further you get from the
middle. I sat on Marion's right the first night, then
found myself being edged further and further away
till I got to the extreme end, when I thought it time to
leave. Another day, and I should have been feeding on
the floor.

P. G. Wodehouse, letter to a friend, 1931

*But there will always be guests whom no hint can shift, or
hosts too polite to hint. Charles Dickens and his family
(his daughter Kate became Mrs Perugini) took the only
means of redress left to them after Hans Christian
Andersen's visit: they told everyone what he had been*

like, and Dickens himself indulged in one pointless but probably highly satisfying gesture of exasperation.

Hans Andersen's scant knowledge of the English language, which he spoke falteringly and with a very broken accent, made it extremely difficult for him to express himself distinctly, or to be adequately understood in conversation; which disadvantage may, in part, have led Mrs Perugini, when asked her opinion of the man, to reply:

'He was a bony bore, and stayed on and on.'

As for Dickens himself, despite his pressing invitation, his acclamation of the Dane's genius, and his untiring exertions to render the visit an enjoyable one, he could not – after his guest's departure – resist the temptation of writing on a card which he stuck up over the dressing-table mirror:

'Hans Andersen slept in this room for five weeks – which seemed to the family AGES!'

Gladys Storey, *Dickens and Daughter*, 1939

Perhaps writers make particularly hazardous guests. Lady Gregory's daughter remembers W. B. Yeats's visits to Coole Park.

Mr Yeats used to stay with us at Coole from as far back as I can remember.

There was a large bed of sedum in the flower garden, by the first vinery; in the summer it was alive with butterflies and I can remember Mamma once saying that sedum flowered all the year round; and while it was in flower Yeats would be at Coole.

Anne Gregory, *Me and Nu : Childhood at Coole*, 1970

Departure & Thanks

The perfect guest, however pained, gives nothing away, not as he leaves, nor in his thanks afterwards. But for less than perfect guests the temptation to relax with escape in sight is strong.

'Well,' said Uncle Fred, as we breakfasted together for what we both devoutly hoped might be the last time, 'you have had a nice long visit. I don't expect we shall see you for a long time now.'

'It's been lovely. I do hope not,' I said, tumbling into the trap. This pleased Uncle Fred so much that he gave me a tip at parting.

Rosemary Edisford, *A Picnic in the Shade*, 1958

The story is told of a guest who was asked to write a parting message in the visitors' book. He inscribed the words: 'Quoth the Raven . . .'

Mr Collins, the insufferably pompous clergyman in Pride and Prejudice *who gave his name to bread-and-butter thank-you letters, here concludes his visit to the Bennet family.*

As he was to begin his journey too early on the morrow to see any of the family, the ceremony of leave-taking was performed when the ladies moved for the night; and Mrs Bennet with great politeness and cordiality said how happy they should be to see him at Longbourn again, whenever his other engagements might allow him to visit them.

'My dear Madam,' he replied, 'this invitation is particularly gratifying, because it is what I have been hoping to receive; and you may be very certain that I shall avail myself of it as soon as possible.'

They were all astonished; and Mr Bennet, who could by no means wish for so speedy a return, immediately said,

'But is there not danger of Lady Catherine's disapprobation here, my good sir? – You had better neglect your relations, than run the risk of offending your patroness.'

'My dear sir,' replied Mr Collins, 'I am particularly obliged to you for this friendly caution, and you may depend upon my not taking so material a step without her ladyship's concurrence.'

'You cannot be too much on your guard. Risk any thing rather than her displeasure; and if you find it likely to be raised by your coming to us again, which I should think exceedingly probable, stay quietly at home, and be satisfied that *we* shall take no offence.'

'Believe me, my dear sir, my gratitude is warmly excited by such affectionate attention; and depend upon it, you will speedily receive from me a letter of thanks for this, as well as for every other mark of your regard during my stay in Hertfordshire ...'

The promised letter of thanks from Mr Collins arrived on Tuesday, addressed to their father, and written with all the solemnity of gratitude which a twelvemonth's abode in the family might have prompted.

Jane Austen, Pride and Prejudice, 1813

These two models for 'a modern bread and butter letter or Collins' appeared in The Weekend Book, *Francis Meynell's compendium of humour, amusements and etiquette for the weekender.*

Dear Molly,

What a week-end! A household like yours shows us

stuffy town-mice just what we miss. All those endless gossips over the washing-up! The romps with the children – dear things, so ready to accept one as their equal! The *smugness* of toasting one's toes at a blaze one has *laboured* to provide. Then that glorious windy climb to your quaint little market town and the lovely long *scribbler's eavesdrop* in the queue before plunging *headlong* home again! (Did I remember to tell you your back brake was broken?) And never did I *dream* I'd be present at the return of a real *prodigal* – so well-timed too, with Vicar there to tea!

Back in my little flat I realise how *right* my doctor was when he said I should enjoy life again after a complete change. Thank you a thousand times for that change.

Yours affectionately,

Dear Pandora,

I got back all right. That was the *slow* train. They took the fast one off last May. My wire hadn't arrived. So Jocelyn must have put 'Highbury' instead of 'Highgate' after all.

Excuse uneven writing – it's the bandage. Which reminds me, could you possibly see if I dropped my bangle in the wood-shed – either there or by the sink? Sorry – it was the rush at the end and the confusion of seeing Francis again after all those years. He's got very Australian, hasn't he?

Hope peace reigns in the nursery today. Sebastian and Sary Ann certainly are wonderfully lively! And I shall always remember my 'Dick Turpin's last ride' on Saturday afternoon. And he wasn't carrying six of gran. and two of lump. Well, thanks so much, Pandora. It was sweet of you to ask me, especially with no help.

Love,

The Weekend Book, 1955

THE FLIGHT TO TOWN

Mrs Lowsborough-Goodby gives weekends,
And her weekends are not a success;
But she asks you so often, you finally soften,
And end by answering 'Yes'.
When I left Mrs Lowsborough-Goodby's,
The letter I wrote was polite;
But it would have been bliss had I dared write her this –
The letter I wanted to write:

'Thank you so much, Mrs *Louse*borough-Goodby, thank
    you so much,
Thank you so much for that infinite weekend with
    you.
Thank you a lot, Mrs *Louse*borough-Goodby,
    thank you a lot;
And don't be surprised if you suddenly should be
    quietly shot!
For the clinging perfume of that damp little room,
For those cocktails so hot, and the bath that was not,
For those guests so amusing and mentally bracing,
Who talked about racing, and racing, and racing,
For the ptomaine I got from your famous tinned
    salmon,
And the fortune I lost when you taught me backgammon,
For those mornings I spent with your dear but deaf
  mother,

For those evenings I passed with that bounder, your
   brother,
And for making me swear to myself there and then
Never to go for a weekend again,
Thank you so much, Mrs *Louse*borough-Goodby,
Thank you, thank you *so much*.'

Cole Porter

A guest's girlfriend, overheard by the hostess:

'Who did you say these people are, darling? I suppose
I'll have to send a thank you note ...'

M. F. K. Fisher, *The Art of Eating*, 1963

*When everything about a visit has been appalling,
consider only that at least it did come to an end. In
Kaufman and Hart's play* The Man Who Came to
Dinner, *the huge, rude and dominating writer Sheridan
Whiteside simply slips on the ice on the doorstep of a
quiet Ohio family. He takes over the household, apparently
or the foreseeable future.*

*More fearsome still is the host whose perfect manners
are marred by only one thing – the guest cannot leave.
Here, Jonathan Harker begins to suspect that this is the
case with Count Dracula.*

'Why may I not go tonight?'

'Because, dear sir, my coachmen and horses are
away on a mission.'

'But I would walk with pleasure. I want to be away
at once.' He smiled, such a soft, smooth, diabolical
smile that I knew there was some trick behind his
smoothness. He said:

'And your baggage?'

'I do not care about it. I can send for it some other
time.'

The count stood up and said, with a sweet courtesy
which made me rub my eyes, it was so real:

[87]

'You English have a saying which is close to my heart, for its spirit is that which rules our *boyars*: "Welcome the coming, speed the parting guest." Come with me, my dear young friend. Not an hour shall you wait in my house against your will, though sad am I at your going, and that you so suddenly desire it. Come!' With a stately gravity, he, with the lamp, preceded me down the stairs and along the hall. Suddenly he stopped.

'Hark!'

Close at hand came the howling of many wolves. It was almost as if the sound sprang up at the raising of his hand. . . . After a pause of a moment he proceeded, in his stately way, to the door, drew back the ponderous bolts, unhooked the heavy chains, and began to draw it open.

To my intense astonishment I saw that it was unlocked. . . .

As the door began to open, the howling of the wolves without grew louder and angrier; their red jaws, with champing teeth, and their blunt-clawed feet as they leaped, came in through the opening door. . . . Suddenly it struck me that this might be the moment and the means of my doom; I was to be given to the wolves, and at my own instigation. There was a diabolical wickedness in the idea great enough for the count, and as a last chance I cried out:

'Shut the door; I shall wait till morning!' and covered my face with my hands to hide my bitter disappointment. With one sweep of his powerful arm, the Count threw the door shut.

Bram Stoker, *Dracula*, 1897

Acknowledgements

An anthologist quickly learns to dread help of the 'I'm sure there's something in Dickens' variety, and so I am particularly grateful to the following for their specific suggestions: Liz Blunt, Hugo Brunner, Mary Rose Brunner, David Cecil, Barbara Cox, Kenneth Dover, John Ezard, Christine Kelly, Penelope Keyte, Margaret Langford, K. M. Lea, Jeremy Lewis, Eric Lusted, Pat McLoughlan, Mary Jane Mowat, Hermann Pálsson, Nigel Rees, Elizabeth Seager, Jane Shaw, Tom Shippey, Maida Stanier, Robert Stanier, Rayner Unwin, Nicholas Woodhouse.

The editor and publishers gratefully acknowledge permission to use copyright material in this book:

Harold Acton: Extracts from *Nancy Mitford, A Memoir* (Hamish Hamilton). Reprinted by permission of David Higham Associates Ltd.

Kingsley Amis: Extract from *Lucky Jim*. Copyright 1953 by Kingsley Amis. Reprinted by permission of Victor Gollancz Ltd., and Doubleday & Co. Inc.

Daisy Ashford: Extract from *The Young Visiters; or, Mr. Salteenas plan*. Reprinted by permission of Chatto & Windus Ltd., for the author's literary estate.

Lady Cynthia Asquith: Extract from *Diaries 1915–18*. Reprinted by permission of Hutchinson General Books Ltd.

W. H. Auden & C. Isherwood: Extract from *Journey to a War*. Reprinted by permission of Faber & Faber Ltd., and Random House, Inc.

Dacre Balsdon: Extract from *Oxford Life* (Eyre & Spottiswoode). Reprinted by permission of David Higham Associates Ltd.

Max Beerbohm: Extract from *Hosts and Guests* (Heinemann). Reprinted by permission of Mrs Eva Reichmann.

Lord David Cecil: Extract from *Two Quiet Lives*. Reprinted by permission of Constable & Co. Ltd., and David Higham Associates Ltd.

Margaret Craven: Extract from *I Heard the Owl Call My Name*. Reprinted by permission of George G. Harrap & Co. Ltd.

Angus Davidson: Extract from *Edward Lear*. Reprinted by permission of John Murray (Publ.) Ltd.

Rosemary Edisford: Extract from *A Picnic In the Shade*. Reprinted by permission of Hutchinson General Books Ltd.

M. F. K. Fisher: Extract from *The Art of Eating* (Faber 1963). Reprinted by permission of A. M. Heath & Co. Ltd., and Russell & Volkening, Inc.

Stella Gibbons: Extract from *Cold Comfort Farm*. Reprinted by permission of David Higham Associates Ltd.

Kenneth Grahame: Extract from *The Wind in the Willows*. Text Copyright University Chest, Oxford. Reprinted by permission of Methuen Children's Books Ltd., and Charles Scribner's Sons.

ACKNOWLEDGEMENTS

Anne Gregory: Extract from *Me and Nu: Childhood at Coole* (1970). Reprinted by permission of Colin Smythe Ltd.

Joyce Grenfell: Extract from *Joyce Grenfell Requests the Pleasure*. Reprinted by permission of Macmillan, London & Basingstoke, and St. Martin's Press, Inc.

L. P. Hartley: Extract from 'A Beautiful Character', Copyright © 1973 the Executors of the Estate of L. P. Hartley, in *Night Fears*, 1924. By permission of Hamish Hamilton, Ltd.

Michael Holroyd: Extract from *Lytton Strachey: A Biography*. Reprinted by permission of Wm. Heinemann Ltd., and Holt, Rinehart & Winston, Inc.

Spike Hughes: Extract from *The Art of Coarse Entertaining*. Reprinted by permission of Hutchinson General Books Ltd.

Philip Larkin: From *High Windows*. Copyright © 1974 by Philip Larkin. Reprinted by permission of Faber & Faber Ltd., and Farrar, Straus & Giroux, Inc.

Marghanita Laski: Extract from *Apologies* (The Harvill Press). Reprinted by permission of David Higham Associates Ltd.

A. G. Macdonell: Extract from *England Their England* (1933). Reprinted by permission of Macmillan, London and Basingstoke.

Francis Meynell: Extracts from *The Weekend Book*. Reprinted by permission of The Bodley Head.

A. A. Milne: Extract from *Winnie the Pooh*. Copyright 1926 by E. P. Dutton & Co., Inc., renewal 1954 by A. A. Milne. Reprinted by permission of Methuen Children's Books, E. P. Dutton, and McClelland and Stewart, Canada.

Jessica Mitford: Extract from *Hons and Rebels*. Reprinted by permission of Victor Gollancz Ltd., and Curtis Brown Ltd.

Marianne Moore: From *The Complete Poems of Marianne Moore*. Copyright 1935 by Marianne Moore, renewed 1963 by Marianne Moore and T. S. Eliot. Reprinted by permission of Faber & Faber Ltd., and Macmillan Publishing Co., Inc.

Robert Morley: Extract from *A Musing Morley* (1974). Reprinted by permission of Robson Books.

Samuel Pepys: Extract from *Diary*, 26 March 1662. Reprinted by permission of A. D. Peters & Co. Ltd.

Cole Porter: 'Thank you so much, Mrs Lowsborough-Goodby', words and music by Cole Porter. Copyright 1934 Harms Inc. (Warner Bros.). Reprinted by kind permission of the British Publisher, Chappell Music Ltd., and Warner Bros., Music, Hollywood.

Beatrix Potter: Extract from *The Tale of Mrs Tittlemouse*. Reprinted by permission of Frederick Warne & Co. Ltd.

Stephen Potter: Extracts from *Lifemanship*. Reprinted by permission of Granada Publishing Ltd., and A. D. Peters & Co. Ltd.

Anthony Powell: Extract from *At Lady Molly's*. Copyright © 1957 by Anthony Powell. Reprinted by permission of Wm. Heinemann Ltd., and Little, Brown, and Co. Extract from *Infants of the Spring*. Reprinted by permission of Wm. Heinemann Ltd., and Holt, Rinehart & Winston, Inc.

Bertrand Russell: Extract from *Autobiography of Bertrand Russell*. Reprinted by permission of George Allen & Unwin.

Edith Sitwell: Extract from *The English Eccentrics* (Dobson). Reprinted by permission of David Higham Associates Ltd.

J. A. Spender: Extract reproduced from *Oxford*, 1936 (The Journal of the Oxford Society). By permission.

J. I. M. Stewart: Extract from *My Oxford* (ed. by Ann Thwaite, 1977). Reprinted by permission of Robson Books.

ACKNOWLEDGEMENTS

Gladys Storey: Extract from *Dickens and Daughter* (1939). Reprinted by permission of Frederick Muller Ltd.

Evelyn Waugh: Extracts from *Vile Bodies*. Copyright 1930 by Evelyn Waugh. Copyright © renewed 1958 by Evelyn Waugh. Extract from *Brideshead Revisited*. Copyright 1944, 1945 by Evelyn Waugh. Copyright © renewed 1972, 1973 by Mrs Laura Waugh. Reprinted by permission of A. D. Peters & Co. Ltd., and Little, Brown, Inc.

Katherine Whitehorn: Extracts from *Whitehorn's Social Survival*. Reprinted by permission of A. D. Peters & Co. Ltd.

P. G. Wodehouse: Extract from *Young Men in Spats* (Herbert Jenkins, 1936); and extract from *Performing Flea, a self-portrait in letters* (Barrie & Jenkins, 1953). Reprinted by permission of A. P. Watt, Ltd.

While every effort has been made to secure permission, we may have failed in a few cases to trace the copyright holder. We apologize for any apparent negligence.

The illustrations in this book were taken from a cartoon by Arthur Watts in *Punch* (1923). Reproduced by courtesy of Punch Magazines.

Index of Authors

Numbers in **bold type** refer to passages in which these names feature

Acton, Harold, 8, **29–30**
Amis, Kingsley, **39–41**
Andersen, Hans Christian, 81
Ashford, Daisy, 2
Ask Mama, 77
Asquith, Lady Cynthia, 9
Asquith, Margot, 9
Aubrey, John, 19
Auden, W. H., **26–7**, **72–3**
Austen, Jane, 75, **83–4**

Balsdon, Dacre, **10–12**
Beerbohm, Max, viii, **44–5**, 74
Bell, Gertrude, 43
Beresford, Lord Charles, 9
Boswell, James, 1, **24–5**
Bowra, Maurice, **56–7**

Carpenter, Humphrey, **26–7**

Cecil, Lord David, 51
Cowper, William, 4
Craven, Margaret, 74
Creevey, Mrs, **49–50**
Creevey, Thomas, **48–9**

Davidson, Angus, 58
De la Mare, Walter, **10**
Dickens, Charles, 8, **62–4**, **81–2**

Eden, Emily, 37, **46–7**
Edisford, Rosemary, 83
Everybody's Everyday Reference Book, 4, **75–6**, 77

Fisher, M. F. K., **28–9**, 87
Franklin, Benjamin, 77

Gaskell, Elizabeth, **69–70**, 76

Gay, John, 64–5
George, Prince Regent, 49–50
Gibbons, Stella, 6–8
Gladstone, William Ewart, 25–6
Gosse, Sir Edmund, 21–2
Grahame, Kenneth, 60–2
Granville, Harriet, Countess of, 22, 37, 50
Gray, Thomas, 51
Gregory, Anne, 82
Grenfell, Joyce, 10, 35
Grossmith, George and Weedon, 31–2

Hartley, L. P., 59–60
Hearst, William Randolph, 81
Heaton, Rose Henniker, 21
Holmes, Oliver Wendell, 21–2
Holroyd, Michael, 66–7
Hook, Theodore, 33–5
Hughes, Spike, 19–20, 73

Isherwood, Christopher, 72–3

Johnson, Samuel, 1, 24–5, 64–5
Jonson, Ben, 1
Jowett, Benjamin, 58

Laboulaye, Edouard, 77
Larkin, Philip, 2–3
Laski, Marghanita, 58–9
Lear, Edward, 58
Louis Philippe, King, 27–8
Louise, Queen, 27–8

Macdonnell, A. G., 16–18
Melbourne, Lord, 50
Meynell, Francis, 73, 84–5
Milne, A. A., 15–16
Mitford, Jessica, 55–6
Mitford, Nancy, 8, 29–30, 55–6
Moore, Marianne, 75
Morley, Robert, 25

Morrell, Lady Ottoline, 56–7

Pain, Barry, 70–1
Pepys, Samuel, 45
Phelps, Lancelot, 78
Plautus, 77
Pope, Alexander, 64–5
Porson, Richard, 38–9
Porter, Adrian, 42
Porter, Cole, 86–7
Post, Emily, 22–3
Potter, Beatrix, 30
Potter, Stephen, 35–7
Powell, Anthony, 56–7, 67–9
Punch, 50

Russell, Bertrand, 25–6

Shakespeare, William, 10
Sitwell, Edith, 38–9
Spender, J. A., 58
Stewart, J. I. M., 78
Stoker, Bram, 87–8
Storey, Gladys, 81–2
Strachey, James, 66–7
Surtees, R. S., 4–6, 79–81
Swift, Jonathan, 64–5

Thackeray, William Makepeace, 1, 24, 72
Tolstoy, Leo, vii
Trefusis, Violet, 29–30
Trollope, Anthony, 47–8

Victoria, Queen, 27–8, 58

Walpole, Horace, 37–8
Waugh, Evelyn, 13–15, 51–3
Wharton, Grace and Philip, 33–5
Whitehorn, Katharine, 24, 78
Wodehouse, P. G., 53–5, 81

Yeats, W. B., 82